PRACTICAL
ACCOUNTING
FOR
SMALL
BUSINESSES

PRACTICAL ACCOUNTING FOR SMALL BUSINESSES

Lyn Taetzsch and Laura Taetzsch, C.P.A.

PETROCELLI / CHARTER   NEW YORK 1977

First Printing

Printed in the United States of America

Library of Congress Cataloging in Publication Data

Taetzsch, Lyn.
    Practical accounting for small businesses.

    Bibliography: p.
    Includes index.
    1. Accounting.   I. Taetzsch, Laura, 1945– joint
author.   II. Title.
HF5635.T15   657'.9042   77-2919
ISBN 0-88405-445-4

CONTENTS

PREFACE

Few individuals starting their own businesses have the knowledge or know-how to set up and utilize accounting records. Yet the success or failure of that business will depend on the ability of the small business manager to gather and evaluate accounting data concerning his business's operations. It is imperative, therefore, that the small business entrepreneur understand the principles of accounting, develop an effective recordkeeping system, and make management decisions based on this feedback.

In *Practical Accounting for Small Businesses,* Laura and Lyn Taetzsch define accounting principles and practices in a clear, easy-to-follow manner. They address the small business entrepreneur directly, presenting the most practical procedures for each accounting area, that is, the simplest methods that will provide the optimum information.

The text begins with a simple explanation of basic accounting theory and continues on to a detailed description of how to set up day-to-day recordkeeping. Step-by-step instructions are given for recording general and specific transactions of all types of businesses on both cash and accrual bases. The special problems of retail and manufacturing accounting are handled in detail in separate chapters.

In the sections on payroll and sales taxes, the authors provide complete information on the legal responsibilities of the small business manager. The reader is given instructions for registering with government agencies, collecting sales taxes, withholding payroll taxes, and filing the necessary city, state and federal forms.

In the chapter on financial statements, the reader is given step-by-step instructions for preparing income statements and balance sheets, with ample illustrations of typical end-of-the-year adjustments. In the section on managerial accounting, the reader learns how to analyze the financial statements in order to obtain valuable feedback on his or her business's performance. The chapter on cash budgeting and financial planning explains how to use this feedback for planning and decision-making.

All in all, the authors have provided a complete guide to the accounting practices of small businesses. I wholeheartedly recommend *Practical Accounting for Small Businesses* as a practical handbook for every small business owner.

Florence Haggis, C.P.A.

1
ACCOUNTING
THEORY

As a small business manager, the use of accounting methods will be valuable to you for three reasons: (a) to provide feedback as to how your business is doing; (b) to provide information for decision making; (c) to provide the records required by the Internal Revenue Service.

The beauty of accounting is that its basic principles can be adapted to a very small business or developed to handle the most complex operations. Although an attempt is made in this book to cover all the common situations a small business might encounter, the principles and systems presented here can be expanded to include other information.

FINANCIAL STATEMENTS

Financial statements are the end products or consolidations of information you will be recording regularly about your business. The simple balance sheet and income statement (sometimes called a ''profit and loss statement'') in Figure 1.1 illustrates how accounting works. To begin our discussion of these statements, let us first define some terms.

Asset. Anything the company owns of monetary value (inventory, cash, equipment, real estate) plus money owed to the company.

Liability. Money the company owes others.

Owner's equity. A company's assets minus liabilities. Put another way, if all the company's assets of $70,000 were used to pay off all the company's liabilities of $40,000, there would be $30,000 left over.

Balance sheet. A statement showing the assets, liabilities, and owner's equity at a particular point in time.

Income statement. A statement showing a company's activity over a period of time, indicating the net profit or loss after cost of goods sold and operating expenses are subtracted from revenues (sales).

Cost of goods sold. In a retail operation, the wholesale price the company paid for the goods it sold; in a manufacturing operation, the total cost of raw materials plus labor and other costs involved in producing the items.

Gross profit. The profit after cost of goods sold is subtracted from sales, before other expenses of running the business are subtracted.

Operating expenses. Any costs incurred during the period in which the revenues were made, but not part of the cost of goods sold. (For example, the $3,000 rent in Figure 1.1 covers the cost of rent for the 12-month period of the statement.)

Net profit. Profit left after subtracting operating expenses from gross profit.

Retained earnings. Profits that are retained in the company as working capital and not distributed to the owners of the company.

The business described in the financial statements in Figure 1.1 is a fictitious retail store that has been in business for two years at the time these statements were prepared. The balance sheet shows what the financial status of the business is at a particular point—the end of 1976. At that time the business has $8,000 in the bank. It has an accounts receivable (money owed the business by its customers) of $15,000. By taking a physical inventory at the end of the year, the company found it had $40,000 worth of goods. And the various equipment it owned (store fixtures, cash registers, delivery truck, etc.) was valued at $7,000 as of that date. This gave the business total assets of $70,000.

On the liability side, the business owed its suppliers $5,000 (accounts payable) and had a bank loan outstanding of $33,000. As of the date of the balance sheet it also owed $2,000 in sales taxes on merchandise it had already sold. This made the company's total liabilities $40,000.

By subtracting the liabilities from the assets, we see that the owner's equity (or net worth) in the business was $30,000 at this time. This $30,000 consists of

BALANCE SHEET AS OF 12/31/76

Assets		Liabilities	
Cash	$ 8,000	Accounts Payable	$ 5,000
Accounts Receivable	15,000	Loan Payable	33,000
Inventory	40,000	Sales Tax Payable	2,000
Equipment	7,000	Total Liabilities	40,000
		Owner's Equity	
		Owner's Capital account	10,000
		Retained Earnings	20,000
Total Assets	$70,000	O.E. + Liabilities	$70,000

INCOME STATEMENT FROM 1/1/76 TO 12/31/76

Sales		$110,000
Cost of Goods Sold		80,000
Gross Profit		30,000
Operating Expenses		
Rent	3,000	
Utilities	500	
Salaries	10,500	
Advertising	2,000	
Insurance	500	
Sales Taxes	3,500	
Total Operating Expenses		20,000
Net Income		$ 10,000
Retained Earnings, Beginning of Year:		10,000
Retained Earnings, End of Year:		$ 20,000

FIGURE 1.1 Two simplified financial statements: A Balance Sheet and an Income Statement (sometimes called a "Profit and Loss Statement"). The Balance Sheet is for a particular point in time (12/31/76) and the Income Statement covers a period of time (1/1/76 to 12/31/76).

$10,000 in the owner's capital account (money he personally invested in the business) and $20,000 of retained earnings. Let us examine the income statement now and see where these retained earnings came from.

The income statement covers a period of time—in our example, the whole year beginning January 1, 1976, and ending December 31, 1976 (the date of the balance sheet). This statement shows how the company earned its profits (or lost its losses).

The first figure listed on the income statement is "sales"—the revenues the company generated throughout the year by its sales efforts. Because this is a retail operation, we next subtract the cost of goods sold—the wholesale price paid for the goods that were sold. This leaves us a gross profit of $30,000.

There are, however, other costs involved in doing business throughout the year in order to make that $110,000 worth of sales. These costs are listed under operating expenses, and in this company's case they came to $20,000. By subtracting the $20,000 from the $30,000 gross profit, we get the net profit of $10,000. This is the amount of money the business made during that year.

The previous year the company also made profits of $10,000, and this is listed as "retained earnings, beginning of year." That $10,000 plus the $10,000 made in 1976 were retained in the company (not paid out to owners) and the total $20,000 made during the two years gives the figure shown on the balance sheet as "retained earnings."

To sum it up, the balance sheet gives a complete financial picture of the company at one point in time. It shows what the business owns, what it owes, and the difference between these, which is owner's equity. An income statement shows the activity that took place during a period of time in order to earn the profits (or losses) which affect the amount of owner's equity on the balance sheet in the form of retained earnings.

THE ACCOUNTING EQUATION

You might have noticed from the example above that

$$\text{assets} = \text{liabilities} + \text{owner's equity}$$

This is called the "accounting equation." The left side of the equation must always equal the right side. If a business has assets of $100,000, for example, the liabilities plus owner's equity must also equal $100,000.

Let us look at a few simple examples to illustrate this point. Suppose you want to start a new business, and you have $50,000 to invest in it. So you open a bank account in the business name and deposit the $50,000. Your business's balance sheet will now be as follows:

Assets		Liabilities	0
Cash	$50,000		
		Owner's Equity	
		Owner's Capital account	$50,000
Total Assets	$50,000	O.E. + Liabilities	$50,000

Let us say you then buy $30,000 worth of inventory. You pay $20,000 cash and agree to pay the other $10,000 in 30 days (creating an accounts payable of $10,000). A look at the balance sheet now shows

Assets		*Liabilities*	
Cash	$30,000	Accounts Payable	$10,000
Inventory	30,000		
		Owner's Equity	
		Owner's Capital account	50,000
Total Assets	$60,000	O.E. + Liabilities	$60,000

Because you spent $20,000 of your cash, you have $30,000 left. There has been an increase in your assets, however, of $30,000 worth of inventory. This transaction has created an accounts payable of $10,000 which is listed as a liability.

Then suppose you take out a bank loan in order to buy $20,000 worth of equipment for your business. Your balance sheet now shows

Assets		*Liabilities*	
Cash	$30,000	Accounts Payable	$10,000
Inventory	30,000	Loans Payable	20,000
Equipment	20,000		
		Owner's Equity	
		Owner's Capital account	50,000
Total assets	$80,000	O.E. + Liabilities	$80,000

Note that the $20,000 in equipment you bought shows as an asset on the balance sheet, and the $20,000 loan is a liability. As we can see from the above examples, no matter what activity your business engages in, the accounting equation always remains balanced:

$$\text{assets} = \text{liabilities} + \text{owner's equity}$$

RECORDING TRANSACTIONS

In the above examples, there were several business transactions: You used cash to buy inventory; you took out a loan; you bought equipment. Whenever your business is involved in receiving or paying out (goods, cash, or even a promise to pay), this is called a "transaction." Since so many transactions occur in the ordinary operations of a business, it would be tedious to draw up a new balance sheet for each. So accountants record these transactions on what are called "T-accounts." They are called this because they resemble a T. A T-account is set up for each asset, liability, or owner's equity account. The following are some examples:

CASH		INVENTORY		LOANS PAYABLE	
debit	credit	debit	credit	debit	credit

In case you are worried about those words "debit" and "credit," rest assured that they mean nothing more than "left" and "right." Debit is always the left side of the T-account and credit is always the right side of the T-account.

To show how transactions are recorded on T-accounts, let us start out with a new business in which the owner invests $100,000. When he deposits this $100,000 in the bank, his balance sheet appears as follows:

Assets		*Liabilities*	0
Cash	$100,000		
		Owner's Equity	
		Owner's Capital account	$100,000
Total Assets	$100,000	O.E. + Liabilities	$100,000

This $100,000 investment is recorded on the following two T-accounts:

CASH		OWNER'S CAPITAL	
debit	credit	debit	credit
100,000			100,000

Note that we increased the Cash account by debiting and the Owner's Capital account by crediting. The rules for increasing accounts are as follows:

Asset accounts are increased by debiting.

Liability accounts are increased by crediting.

Owner's Equity accounts are increased by crediting.

And the opposite is true:

Asset accounts are decreased by crediting.

Liability accounts are decreased by debiting.

Owner's Equity accounts are decreased by debiting.

Shown diagramatically,

Assets	=	Liabilities + Owner's Equity
plus (+) = debit (left)		plus (+) = credit (right)
minus (−) = credit (right)		minus (−) = debit (left)

In this way the accounting equation is kept in balance. Every transaction will always involve at least two T-accounts, and if the amount is entered as a debit on one account, it must be entered as a credit on the other.

There are various kinds of transactions. Some, for example, simply exchange one kind of asset for another. This would happen if $30,000 in cash were used to buy $30,000 worth of inventory. Cash would be decreased (credited) and Inventory would be increased (debited):

(asset account)		(asset account)	
CASH		INVENTORY	
debit (+)	credit (−)	debit (+)	credit (−)
* 100,000	30,000	30,000	

Note that the balance in the Cash account (debits minus credits) is now $70,000. Both Cash and Inventory are asset accounts, and therefore this transaction has not changed the total amounts of the left and right sides of the accounting equation on the balance sheet:

Assets		Liabilities	0
Cash	$ 70,000		
Inventory	30,000	Owner's Equity	
		Owner's Capital account	$100,000
Total Assets	$100,000	O.E. + Liabilities	$100,000

In another type of transaction we increase both sides of the equation. Suppose $10,000 worth of supplies is purchased on credit, payable within 30 days. These supplies are an addition to the business's assets, but they also add a liability of an accounts payable:

(asset account)		(liability account)	
SUPPLIES		ACCOUNTS PAYABLE	
debit (+)	credit (−)	debit (−)	credit (+)
10,000			10,000

* Prior entry.

7

Looking at the balance sheet again, we now see

Assets		Liabilities	
Cash	$ 70,000	Accounts Payable	$ 10,000
Inventory	30,000		
Supplies	10,000	*Owner's Equity*	
		Owner's Capital account	100,000
Total Assets	$110,000	O.E. + Liabilities	$110,000

By adding $10,000 worth of supplies to the assets and $10,000 worth of accounts payable to the liabilities, we increased both sides of the equation by $10,000.

In another type of transaction we simply exchange one liability for another, which leaves the total of both sides of the equation the same. Suppose the owner offers to give a note for $5,000 to the company he bought the supplies from in order to reduce his accounts payable to $5,000. This is how the T-accounts would look:

(liability account) ACCOUNTS PAYABLE		(liability account) NOTES PAYABLE	
debit (−)	credit (+)	debit (−)	credit (+)
5,000	* 10,000		5,000

Note that the balance in Accounts Payable (credits minus debits) is now $5,000. Let us see how this transaction looks on the balance sheet:

Assets		Liabilities	
Cash	$ 70,000	Accounts Payable	$ 5,000
Inventory	30,000	Notes Payable	5,000
Supplies	10,000		
		Owner's Equity	
		Owner's Capital account	100,000
Total Assets	$110,000	O.E. + Liabilities	$110,000

In another type of transaction we *decrease* both sides of the equation. Suppose $5,000 cash is used to pay off the $5,000 of accounts payable. This is recorded on T-accounts as

(asset account) CASH		(liability account) ACCOUNTS PAYABLE	
debit (+)	credit (−)	debit (−)	credit (+)
† 100,000	† 30,000	† 5,000	† 10,000
	5,000	5,000	

* Prior entry.
† Prior entries.

Note that the Cash balance (debits minus credits) is now $65,000 and the Accounts Payable balance (credits minus debits) is now zero. The following shows how the transaction affects the balance sheet:

Assets		Liabilities	
Cash	$ 65,000	Notes Payable	5,000
Inventory	30,000		
Supplies	10,000	Owner's Equity	
		Owner's Capital account	100,000
Total Assets	$105,000	O.E. + Liabilities	$105,000

Note that the assets have been decreased by $5,000 cash and the liabilities have been decreased by $5,000 accounts payable.

RECORDING REVENUES

We note that none of the above transactions affected owner's equity. The only way to affect owner's equity is to generate sales, incur expenses, or add or withdraw capital. When revenues (sales) are generated, both the income statement and the balance sheet are affected. Let us assume the above company makes a credit sale of $10,000. The cost of goods sold is $7,000, leaving a profit of $3,000 (we will not worry about operating costs in this example). In order to record this transaction, four (rather than two) T-accounts are used:

(asset account)		(income statement account)	
ACCOUNTS RECEIVABLE		SALES	
debit (+)	credit (−)	debit (−)	credit (+)
10,000			10,000

(asset account)		(income statement account)	
INVENTORY		COST OF GOODS SOLD	
debit (+)	credit (−)	debit (+)	credit (−)
* 30,000	7,000	7,000	

Note that Revenues or Sales accounts are increased by crediting. Other income statement accounts such as Cost of Goods Sold and all operating expenses such as Rent, Salaries, Utilities, Advertising, and Insurance Expense are increased by debiting. In all double-entry recordkeeping, of course, a figure entered on the left

* Prior entry.

9

side of one account must be entered on the right side of it's matching account, and vice versa.

So the $10,000 sale on account is entered on the left (debit) side of Accounts Receivable (an asset because it is money owed the business) and the right (credit) side of Sales. We used up $7,000 worth of inventory, however, to make this sale, decreasing the Inventory account by entering this amount on the right (credit) side. The same $7,000 is listed on the left (debit) side of Cost of Goods Sold.

Let us look at the balance sheet and income statement immediately after this transaction:

BALANCE SHEET

Assets		Liabilities	
Cash	$ 65,000	Notes Payable	$ 5,000
Inventory	23,000		
Supplies	10,000	*Owner's Equity*	
Accounts		Owner's Capital account	100,000
Receivable	10,000	Retained Earnings	3,000
		Total O.E.	103,000
Total Assets	$108,000	O.E. + Liabilities	$108,000

INCOME STATEMENT

Sales	$10,000
Cost of Goods Sold	7,000
Profit	$ 3,000

Retained Earnings: $3,000

Note first the changes on the balance sheet. Inventory was reduced from $30,000 to $23,000 because $7,000 of it was used in the $10,000 sale. Accounts receivable of $10,000 were added to the balance sheet as an asset. This decrease of $7,000 and increase of $10,000 made a net increase on the asset side of $3,000, bringing the total from the previous $105,000 to $108,000.

On the right side of the balance sheet, $3,000 in retained earnings was added to the owner's equity, again bringing the total of owner's equity and liabilities from $105,000 to $108,000. The $3,000 in retained earnings is the profit from the $10,000 sale, as shown on the Income Statement. Sales minus cost of goods sold equals the $3,000 profit.

In this chapter accounting theory has been presented in a nutshell. The rest is simply an expansion of the above principles. If you have found it difficult to grasp the theory in one gulp, however, you should go on to the next chapters, in which more detailed illustrations of the use of this theory will be given. You can then come back and reread this chapter, and you will find that it makes more sense as you see the practical applications.

2
SETTING UP
AND
USING
JOURNALS
AND
LEDGERS

In Chapter 1 we saw how the financial transactions of a business are recorded in T-accounts. The type and number of accounts used will depend on the nature of the business and whether it is on the cash or accrual basis of accounting for tax purposes.

Keeping records on a cash basis means you record income and expenditures at the time you receive or pay out cash. When you pay the rent, write a payroll check, deposit payroll taxes, or pay a supplier for materials, you record a rent expense, salary expense, payroll tax expense, and supplies expense.

If you keep records on an accrual basis, you record income when earned, even if you do not actually receive payment. For example, if you bill a customer for $100 in July and receive payment in August, the $100 is considered part of July sales (on the cash basis it would be considered part of August sales). Similarly, expenses are recorded when incurred, whether or not they are paid at that time. For example, if you receive $500 worth of merchandise in March which you pay for in April, the $500 is charged as an expense in March, not April.

The Internal Revenue Service requires that you choose one of the above accounting methods—cash or accrual—and use it consistently from year to year. The main point to consider in choosing one or the other method is that it truly reflects the income of your business. In general, if the production, purchase, or sale of inventories is an income-producing factor (as it is in retail and manufacturing), you will use the accrual method. A service business might find the cash method easiest to use. It will also accurately reflect income.

You may want to use a combination of methods that will suit your particular needs. Since the cash basis is simpler, some companies keep their daily records with this method, making adjustments at the end of the year to fit the accrual method. In the chapters that follow, systems for cash and accrual will be presented, depending on the particular situation.

A LIST OF T-ACCOUNTS

The following T-accounts are typical ones used by many businesses. Receivables and Payables accounts refer to the accrual method of accounting. Receivables is money owed your company and Payables is money you owe others. This list does not include special accounts for retail and manufacturing companies such as inventory and cost of goods sold. (See individual chapters for specific information.)

Asset Accounts. Asset accounts are increased by debiting, decreased by crediting.

> *Cash.* Includes all cash held by the business in checking accounts, petty cash, cash registers, etc.

> *Accounts receivable.* Sales that have been invoiced (for goods shipped or services rendered) but the customer has not yet paid for.

> *Notes receivable.* Sum of outstanding money owed the company in the form of notes or promises to pay.

> *Property.* Buildings, land, or other real estate owned and used by the business.

> *Equipment.* Machinery and other equipment owned by the business.

> *Vehicles.* Trucks, cars, and other vehicles owned by the business.

Liability Accounts. Liability accounts are increased by crediting, decreased by debiting.

> *Accounts payable.* Money the company owes others for goods or services already received.

> *Notes payable.* Outstanding notes and loans the company owes.

14

Sales taxes payable. Sales taxes the company owes on goods already sold.

Payroll taxes payable. Payroll taxes the company has not yet paid but owes for work already performed. (For example, if a company is required to deposit payroll taxes every three months, at the end of one month the Payroll Taxes Payable account will include taxes owed on the salaries paid out that month.)

Owner's Equity Accounts. Owner's equity accounts keep track of the capital invested and withdrawn from the company by owners, plus the earnings retained by the company. These accounts are increased by crediting and decreased by debiting.

Owner's capital account. The balance of the capital an owner has invested in the business. (In a partnership, there will be an owner's capital account for each partner.)

Retained earnings. At the end of each year, any earnings the company retains (not distributed to owners, stockholders, etc.)

Income Statement Accounts: Revenues. Revenues are increased by crediting, decreased by debiting.

Sales. Revenues earned through sales, as opposed to other income such as rents.

Income Statement Accounts: Operating Expenses. Operating Expense accounts keep track of the cost of doing business. You will want to keep an account for each major expense area, plus a Miscellaneous Expense account for small items that do not justify an account of their own. Operating expense accounts are increased by debiting and decreased by crediting.

Salaries expense. Money paid to employees for services.

Payroll tax expense. Payroll taxes paid.

Rent expense. Rent on the building in which a company is doing business.

Utilities expense. Cost of heat, lighting, phone, etc.

Insurance expense. Liability, comprehensive, and other insurance premiums paid by the business.

Interest expense. Interest paid on notes and loans.

Supplies expense. Payments for supplies used by the business.

Miscellaneous expense. Items that do not fall under the above headings.

GENERAL LEDGER

The total group of T-accounts that you set up for your business's recordkeeping is called the "General Ledger." There are various systems available (see Chapter 17) for keeping a general ledger of accounts. Figure 2.1 illustrates a T-account set up on lined columnar pad paper. Note that there are columns for listing the date and description as well as the amount of each debit or credit.

Entering all a business's daily financial transactions in the General Ledger as they occur poses several problems. First, it would be tedious to search through the General Ledger for the appropriate accounts each time you had a transaction to record. Second, you might forget to record each transaction properly as a debit on one account and a credit on its corresponding account. Third, you would have no chronological record of the business's activities easily observable in one place. For these reasons you will want to keep a Cash Disbursements Journal (where all outgoing cash is recorded), a Cash Receipts Journal (where all incoming money is recorded), and a General Journal (to record all other transactions). These journals are kept on a day-to-day basis as transactions occur. Then once a month the information is posted in total to the general ledger (T-accounts).

CASH DISBURSEMENTS JOURNAL

Whenever your business spends money, you will list it in the Cash Disbursements Journal. Figure 2.2 is an example of how a page in a typical Cash Dis-

FIGURE 2.1 A "Sales" T-account. Debit items are recorded on the left side and credit items on the right.

SALES

date	item		debit	date	item		credit

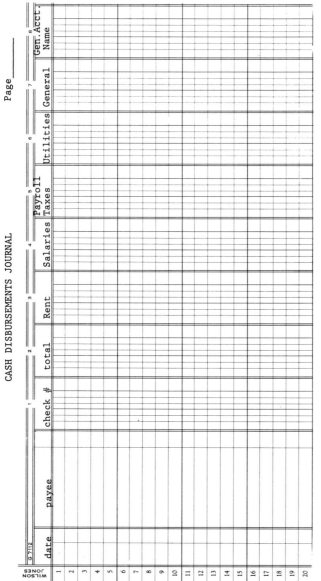

FIGURE 2.2 Page from a Cash Disbursements Journal with separate columns for rent, salaries, payroll taxes, and utilities. Set up Cash Disbursements Journal to fit individual needs.

17

bursements Journal should be set up. Note that there is a place to record the date, the payee, the check number, and the total amount. Then on the right you will want a column for each major disbursement area, such as Rent, Salaries, Payroll Taxes, and Utilities. Columns called "General" and "General Account Name" will be used to list items that do not have a separate column heading.

Every day as you write checks you will record each item in the Cash Disbursements Journal. Check numbers should be listed in order, including voided checks, to be sure none are omitted. The "Payee" will be the name of the person, or company, to whom the check is made out. The total amount of the check should be listed under "total" and then again in the proper account column. If it is a general item, the applicable account name is written under General Account Name. (See Figure 2.3, which illustrates the recording of several typical transactions.)

At the end of the month you will total the columns in the Cash Disbursements Journal as shown in Figure 2.4. Note that the sum of the Rent, Salaries, Payroll Taxes, Utilities, and General columns equal the sum of the "total" column. You are now ready to post these totals in your General Ledger. The total amount of the cash disbursements for the month should be listed as a credit in the Cash account. List the rent total as a debit in the Rent account, salaries as a debit in the Salaries account, and so forth. Each time you make an entry, put a red check mark next to the number in the Cash Disbursements Journal so you will know it has been posted.

Each item in the general column will have to be posted individually to the proper account and each amount checked off as you post it to avoid duplicate posting (see Figure 2.5).

Looking at the Salaries T-account shown in Figure 2.6, we see that a column called "folio" has been added. When posting an item from the Cash Disbursements Journal into the General Ledger, you should make a note under "folio" as to where you got this information. In the example shown, the amount was taken from CD-2, the second page of the Cash Disbursements Journal. If you post an item from other journals, such as the Cash Receipts Journal, you would list this information under "folio" in a similar manner. This way you can always check back to see where information was obtained.

Figure 2.7 shows a sample Cash Disbursements monthly summary. These totals are posted to General Ledger accounts in Figure 2.8. "CD-3" is marked in the folio column of each ledger entry to indicate that the information was taken from the third page of the Cash Disbursements Journal. Note that the total cash disbursements are credited to Cash and debited to each of the expense accounts involved.

18

CASH DISBURSEMENTS JOURNAL   Page 3

	date	payee	check#	total	Rent	Salar.	Payroll tax	Utilit.	Gener.	Gen. Acct Name
1	4 1	A. Markum	2034	450 -	450 -					
2	4 2	United Bank	2035	143.25			143.25			
3	4 4	Office Supply Co.	2036	14.95					14.95	office Sup.
4	4 4	Void	2037							
5	4 6	Bell Tel.	2038	61.80				61.80		
6										
7										
8										
9										
10										
11										
12										
13										
14										
15										
16										
17										
18										
19										
20										

FIGURE 2.3 Page from a Cash Disbursements Journal showing several entries. Note that the office supplies payment of $14.95 is listed under "general."

19

	date	payee	check#	total	Rent	Salar.	Payroll tax	Utili.	General	Gen. Acct Name
1	4 17	J. C. Power Co.	2078	59 35				59 35		
2	4 20	Local Gas	2079	10 95					10 95	Fuel Ex.
3	4 26	L. Benson	2080	242 30		242 30				
4		R. Smith	2081	238 70		238 70				
5	4 30	General Tool Co.	2082	97 30					97 30	Tools Ex.
6				2084 11 ✓	450 - ✓	973 40 ✓	143 25 ✓	166 45 ✓	351 01	
7										
8										
9										
10										
11										
12										
13										
14										
15										
16										
17										
18										
19										
20										

FIGURE 2.4 Page from a Cash Disbursements Journal showing monthly totals. Note the check marks next to the monthly amounts in the total, rent, salaries, payroll taxes, and utilities columns. These check marks mean the amounts have been posted to the General Ledger accounts.

	date	payee	check#	total	Rent	Salar.	Payroll tax	Utili.	General	Gen. Acct Name
1	4 17	J.C. Power Co.	2078	5935				5935		
2	4 20	Local Gas	2079	1095					1095	Fuel Ex.
3	4 26	L. Benson	2080	24230		24230				
4		R. Smith	2081	23876		23876				
5	4 30	General Tool Co.	2082	9730					9730	Tools Ex.
6				2084 11 ✓	450 — ✓	97340 ✓	14325 ✓	16645 ✓	35101	
7										
8										
9										
10										
11										
12										
13										
14										
15										
16										
17										
18										
19										
20										

FIGURE 2.5 This is the same Cash Disbursements Journal page as Figure 2.4. Note that the two items listed in the general column have been checked off to indicate they have been posted to the General Ledger accounts.

21

SALARIES EXPENSE

DATE 19__		I T E M S	FOLIO	√	DEBITS		DATE 19__		I T E M S	FOLIO	√	CREDITS	
2	28	Feb. Payroll	CD-2		825 60								

FIGURE 2.6 Salaries Expense account with "CD-2" written under the "folio" column to indicate that the February payroll amount of $825.60 was taken from page 2 of the Cash Disbursements Journal.

22

	date	payee	check#	total	Salar.	sup.	general	gen.Acct name
1	4 3	Bell Tel.	3029	62 30			62 30	Tel. Ex.
2		VOID	3030					
3	4 15	L. Markowitz	3031	425 -	425 -			
4		J. Mendem	3032	389 -	389 -			
5		J. Johnson	3033	398 -	398 -			
6	4 20	Ace Co.	3034	215 -		215 -		
7	4 23	Ok Ins. Co.	3035	52 -			52 -	Ins. Ex.
8	4 25	Elloy Co.	3036	150 -		150 -		
9	4 30	Lease - H-Bldg. Co.	3037	600 -			600 -	Rent Ex.
10		L. Markowitz	3038	425 -	425 -			
11		J. Mendem	3039	389 -	389 -			
12		J. Johnson	3040	398 -	398 -			
13				3503 30	2424 - ✓	365 - ✓	714 30 ✓	
14								
15								
16								
17								
18								
19								
20								

FIGURE 2.7 Monthly totals on this Cash Disbursements Journal have been posted to the General Ledger accounts illustrated in Figure 2.8.

CASH

DATE 19__	ITEMS	FOLIO	√	DEBITS	DATE 19__	ITEMS	FOLIO	√	CREDITS
					4 30	April Disbursements	CD-3		35 03 30

SALARIES EXPENSE

DATE 19__	ITEMS	FOLIO	√	DEBITS	DATE 19__	ITEMS	FOLIO	√	CREDITS
4 30	April Payroll	CD-3		24 24 —					

SUPPLIES EXPENSE

DATE 19__	ITEMS	FOLIO	√	DEBITS	DATE 19__	ITEMS	FOLIO	√	CREDITS
4 30	April Purchases	CD-3		3 65 —					

24

TELEPHONE EXPENSE

DATE 19__	ITEMS	FOLIO	√	DEBITS	DATE 19__	ITEMS	FOLIO	√	CREDITS
4 30	April	cd-3		62 30					

INSURANCE EXPENSE

DATE 19__	ITEMS	FOLIO	√	DEBITS	DATE 19__	ITEMS	FOLIO	√	CREDITS
4 30	April Payment	cd-3		52 00					

RENT EXPENSE

DATE 19__	ITEMS	FOLIO	√	DEBITS	DATE 19__	ITEMS	FOLIO	√	CREDITS
4 30	April Payment	cd-3		600 —					

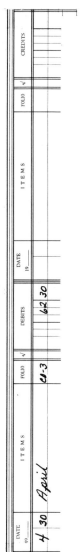

FIGURE 2.8 Entries in these General Ledger accounts were taken from page 3 of the Cash Disbursements Journal shown in Figure 2.7.

25

CASH RECEIPTS JOURNAL

Whenever your business receives money, you will list it in the Cash Receipts Journal. Normally cash receipts will be daily cash sales (if you sell merchandise or services on credit, see Chapter 4). Miscellaneous cash receipts might include refunds from suppliers, rent payments if the business has tenants, and note payments if the business has notes receivable. Figure 2.9 illustrates a page in a typical Cash Receipts Journal. It works in basically the same way as does the Cash Disbursements Journal. The total cash is listed, then either the Sales column is filled in, or the General column, with an explanation. In this example there was a refund from a supplier and a tax refund. All the other cash receipts were from cash sales.

As you did with the Cash Disbursements Journal, at the end of the month you will total your Cash Receipts columns and post the totals to the General Ledger. The amount in the total column is debited to Cash and credited to Sales and whatever general accounts are listed. In the example shown in Figure 2.9, the supplier refund would be credited to Supplies Expense and the tax refund would be credited to Tax Expense.

Figure 2.10 illustrates a Cash Receipts Journal that has been totaled for the month and posted to General Ledger accounts in Figure 2.11. Note that each total or general item has been checked on the Cash Receipts Journal to indicate that it has been posted. "CR-6" has been written in the folio column of the Ledger entries to show that this is where the figure was taken from. Since the total cash received is always debited to Cash, the corresponding entries in the Ledger accounts must be credited.

GENERAL JOURNAL

A General Journal is used to record transactions other than cash receipts or cash disbursements. In a small business the majority of all transactions will involve the flow of cash in or out, so the Cash Receipts and Disbursements Journals will take care of the day-to-day activities of the business.

Actually, all you will probably need will be a single sheet of paper set up as shown in Figure 2.12. It provides a place to record the date, a description of the item, and the accounts that will be debited and credited.

Normally the kind of transactions you will record on the General Journal will only need to be done when you prepare your financial statements (see Chapter 12). Typical items are depreciation of buildings and equipment, prepaid expenses, prepaid insurance, etc.

26

CASH RECEIPTS JOURNAL   Page   1

	date		item			① total	② sales	③ general	④ gen.acct. name
1	5	3	Daily Receipts			201 –	201 –		
2	5	4	" "			215 –	215 –		
3	5	5	" "			198 –	198 –		
4	5	6	" "			220 –	220 –		
5			Marko Co.			20 –		20 –	Supplies Ex
6	5	7	Daily Receipts			230 –	230 –		
7	5	8	" "			220 –	220 –		
8	5	10	" "			175 –	175 –		
9			IRS			5 –		5 –	Tax Ex.
10									
11									
12									
13									
14									
15									
16									
17									
18									
19									
20									

FIGURE 2.9 Cash Receipts Journal showing several entries. The $20 from Marko Company is a refund that will be credited (subtracted) to the Supplies Expense account.

The kind of transaction you may want to record during the year would be something such as a bad debt. It would be preferable to write this loss off when it happened, rather than waiting until you prepare financial statements. For example, suppose you were paid for your services with a check for $100. When you deposited the check in your bank, it did not clear, and you were unable to get the customer to make good on it. This $100 then became a loss. Yet when you made the sale and received the check, you had recorded it as income in your Cash Receipts Journal and it was posted to Cash and Sales in the General Ledger. Now, therefore, you want to write it off as a loss. In fact, you will have to do this in order to reconcile Cash (see Chapter 9) since the bank will charge you for the $100.

Figure 2.13 illustrates how you would record this transaction on your General Journal sheet. At the end of the month any items in the General Journal are posted to the General Ledger as you did with the Cash Receipts and Cash Disbursements Journals.

CASH RECEIPTS JOURNAL   Page   6

	date	item	① total	② sales	③ general	④ gen.acct. name
1	7 1	Daily Receipts	201	201		
2	2	" "	215	215		
3	3	" "	198	198		
4	5	" "	220	220		
5	6	" "	230	230		
6	7	" "	220	220		
7	8	" "	175	175		
8	9	" "	240	240		
9	10	" "	235	235		
10	12	" "	180	180		
11		Marko Co.	20		20 ✓	Supplies Ex
12	13	Daily Receipts	175	175		
13	14	" "	190	190		
14	15	" "	193	193		
15	16	" "	200	200		
16	17	" "	240	240		
17	19	" "	190	190		
18	20	" "	192	192		
19		IRS	5		5 ✓	Payroll Ex
20	21	Daily Receipts	175	175		
21	22	" "	201	201		
22		ARCO Products	23		23 ✓	Supplies Ex
23	23	Daily Receipts	232	232		
24	24	" "	220	220		
25	26	" "	170	170		
26	27	" "	165	165		
27	28	" "	180	180		
28	29	" "	192	192		
29	30	" "	195	195		
30	31	" "	203	203		
3			5475 ✓	5427 ✓	48	
4						
5						

FIGURE 2.10 Page from a Cash Receipts Journal showing monthly totals that are posted to the General Ledger accounts illustrated in Figure 2.11. Note the check marks indicating items have been posted.

CASH

DATE 19__	ITEMS	FOLIO	√	DEBITS		DATE 19__	ITEMS	FOLIO	√	CREDITS
7 31	July Receipts	CR-6		5475						

SALES

DATE 19__	ITEMS	FOLIO	√	DEBITS		DATE 19__	ITEMS	FOLIO	√	CREDITS
						7 31	July Sales	CR-6		5427

SUPPLIES EXPENSE

DATE 19__	ITEMS	FOLIO	√	DEBITS		DATE 19__	ITEMS	FOLIO	√	CREDITS
						7 12	Marto Co. Refund	CR-6		20
						7 22	Arco Products Returns	CR-6		23

PAYROLL EXPENSE

DATE 19__	ITEMS	FOLIO	√	DEBITS		DATE 19__	ITEMS	FOLIO	√	CREDITS
						7 20	IRS - Tax Refund	CR-6		5

FIGURE 2.11 Entries posted in these General Ledger accounts taken from page 6 of the Cash Receipts Journal illustrated in Figure 2.10.

GENERAL JOURNAL   Page _____

	date	description	debit	credit
1				
2				
3				
4				
5				
6				
7				
8				
9				
10				
11				
12				
13				
14				
15				
16				
17				
18				

FIGURE 2.12 Illustration showing how a General Journal should be set up, with columns for date, description, debit, and credit.

GENERAL JOURNAL   Page 1

	date	description	debit	credit
1	7 16	Bad Debt Expense	100 -	
2		Cash		100 -
3		To write off bad		
4		check from D. Dewald		
5				
6				
7				
8				
9				
10				
11				
12				
13				
14				
15				

FIGURE 2.13 General Journal entry made to write off a bad debt. Always list the account to be debited (Bad Debt Expense) first, then the account to be credited (Cash).

SUMMING UP

In this chapter you saw that a Cash Receipts Journal and Cash Disbursements Journal should be used to record the daily flow of money in and out of your business. Any other transaction, such as the loss from a bad debt, is recorded in a General Journal.

Once a month these journals should be totaled, and the totals posted to the General Ledger, which will consist of all the T-accounts applicable to your business: Cash, Sales, Salaries Expense, Rent Expense, Utilities Expense, etc.

If you sell merchandise or services on credit, see Chapter 4 to find out how to invoice your customers, keep a sales journal, write up credit memos, post to general and subsidiary ledgers, and prepare a trial balance of your accounts receivable.

If you have a retail business, see Chapter 5 on procedures for recording inventories and cost of goods sold. If you are a manufacturer, see Chapter 6 on accounting for manufacturing expenses.

3
PURCHASES
AND
ACCOUNTS
PAYABLE

In this chapter you will find three methods for handling your company's purchases. Method 1 is for all companies that keep their records on a cash basis of accounting. If you are on an accrual basis (see Chapter 2 for explanation), you can use either method 2 or 3.

PURCHASE ORDERS

Whichever method you use to record purchases, the first step to keeping track of monies spent on supplies, raw materials, finished goods, etc., is to use numbered purchase order forms (see Figure 3.1). By ordering *everything* through purchase orders you will have better control. For example, you will know on what date you ordered an item, the quantity, the price, and so forth. It gives your supplier complete information about what you want, when you want it, and how you want it shipped. When you recieve the order, you can check to see that what you got is what you ordered.

Purchase order forms are available in various layouts, in carbon sets, and can be imprinted with your name and address. It is best to get forms that are consecutively numbered. That way you can keep a numerical file of all orders. The *purchase order*

PURCHASE ORDER

No. **3615**

Date _____ 19 _____

For _____

To _____ Req. No. _____

Address _____ How Ship _____

City _____ Date Required _____

Ship To _____ Terms _____

QUANTITY		PLEASE SUPPLY ITEMS LISTED BELOW	PRICE	UNIT
ORDERED	RECEIVED			
1				
2				
3				
4				
5				
6				

IMPORTANT

OUR ORDER NUMBER MUST APPEAR ON ALL INVOICES, PACKAGES, ETC.
PLEASE NOTIFY US IMMEDIATELY IF YOU ARE UNABLE TO SHIP COMPLETE ORDER BY DATE SPECIFIED.

Please Send _____ Copies Of Your Invoice With Original Bill Of Lading

Purchasing Agent

1S 144 Rediform®
Poly Pak (50 sets) 1P 144

ORIGINAL

FIGURE 3.1 A purchase order form that can be ordered from the suppliers listed in Chapter 17.

original purchase order goes to the supplier and you will need one or more copies for your records. Forms are available at your local office supply store or can be ordered from the suppliers listed in Chapter 17.

Figure 3.2 is an example of how to fill out a purchase order form. Your company name and address should be typed or printed at the top. The supplier's name and address appears after "to." After "ship to," write in "above" or list your shipping address if it is different from your address at the top of the form (you may have a warehouse or stores at different locations).

The date is the date on which you place the order. "For" and "requisition number" were left blank in this example. After "how ship" you list UPS, parcel post, or the name of a trucking company, unless you want to leave the shipping method up to the supplier. After "date required" put the date on which you want the goods delivered.

"Terms" will usually be up to the supplier unless you are an important customer. You may have to send a check with your order (cash terms) if you are a

PURCHASE ORDER

JONES BAKERY
110 Main Street
Anywhere, U.S.A. 10000

No. **3616**

Date_____ June 1 _____19 77

For _____

To ___Zippy Box Co._____   Req. No._____

Address ___666 Main St._____   How Ship___UPS_____

City ___Anywhere, U.S.A. 10000___   Date Required___June 20th___

Ship To _____above_____   Terms___COD_____

QUANTITY		PLEASE SUPPLY ITEMS LISTED BELOW	PRICE		UNIT
ORDERED	RECEIVED				
1 500		#348 cake boxes	8	00	100
2 1000		#252 donut boxes	7	50	100
3					
4					
5					
6					

IMPORTANT
OUR ORDER NUMBER MUST APPEAR ON ALL INVOICES, PACKAGES, ETC.
PLEASE NOTIFY US IMMEDIATELY IF YOU ARE UNABLE TO SHIP COMPLETE ORDER BY DATE SPECIFIED.

Please Send   2   Copies Of Your Invoice With Original Bill Of Lading

Kathy Jones   Purchasing Agent

1S 144 Rediform®
Poly Pak (50 sets) 1P 144 .

ORIGINAL

FIGURE 3.2 A purchase order filled out by Kathy Jones of Jones Bakery.

new customer and have not established a credit rating. An alternative is "C.O.D.," which stands for "Cash on Delivery." In this case you pay for the goods when you receive them. However, once you establish a good credit rating or a reputation with your supplier, you may be able to purchase merchandise on credit. "Net 30 days," for example, would allow you 30 days to pay for the merchandise after you received it. Some suppliers offer discounts for early payment, such as "2% 10 net 30." This means if you pay within 10 days you can take two percent off the invoice total; otherwise you must pay the whole amount within 30 days.

Note that in the sample purchase order there is a column to list the quantity ordered and the quantity received. This allows you to compare the amount received against the amount ordered when the goods arrive. By listing the price on the purchase order, you alert the supplier as to what you expect to pay. If prices have gone up, the supplier should notify you of the change before shipping your order.

METHOD 1: CASH BASIS

The cash basis of accounting for purchases simply means that you record items when you pay for them. For example, if you sent a purchase order to the Smith Company for office supplies, you would enter the amount as office supplies expense in your Cash Disbursements Journal *when* you pay for them, whether you do so when you place the order, when you receive the goods (COD), or 30 days later. It does not matter when you order or receive the goods, only when you *pay* for them.

Figure 3.3 shows a Cash Disbursements Journal with entries made for payment of three separate purchases: office supplies, printing expenses, and fuel expenses. At the end of the month these columns will be totaled and posted to the General Ledger expense accounts.

METHOD 2: MODIFIED CASH-ACCRUAL

The accrual method of accounting for purchases takes into consideration the fact that you may have in your possession goods or materials for which you have not yet paid. If you buy large quantities of supplies, raw materials, or finished goods on credit, this method will more accurately reflect your situation on financial statements.

For example, suppose you order $30,000 worth of raw materials on 60-day credit terms. If you made up a balance sheet of your company's worth before you paid for those goods, you would include them as part of your assets. This would not be an accurate picture of your company's financial position, however, unless you also listed the $30,000 debt as a liability called "Accounts Payable." After you pay the $30,000, you no longer list it as a liability, but your cash assets will have been reduced by $30,000.

The modified cash–accrual method allows you to record purchases on a cash basis in the day-to-day operation of your business. When you pay an invoice for supplies, raw materials, finished goods, or whatever, you record the amount in your Cash Disbursements Journal as in method 1 above. At the end of the year when you do your financial statements, however, you make an adjustment to reflect a true picture of your situation.

To make this end-of-the-year adjustment, you collect all the outstanding invoices (bills) for goods received but not paid for. These are entered in your General Journal as debits to the applicable expense accounts and credits to Accounts Payable. You then post to your General Ledger accounts. Now your General Ledger accounts will accurately reflect the status of your purchases on an accrual basis.

36

45-164 EYE-EASE
45-464 20/20 BUFF

date	payee	check#	total	salar.	rent	printing	off sup.	fuel	general	gen. acct. name
3 6	Office Supply Corp.	2034	54				54			
3 10	Jiffy Printers	2035	120			120				
3 15	Easy Gas	2036	25					25		

FIGURE 3.3 Page from a Cash Disbursements Journal showing the recording of payments for several purchases.

37

Let us look at a sample situation. The XYZ Company owes $14,500 to various suppliers for goods received as of December 31, 1976. An itemization is as follows:

Invoice from	For	In amount of
ABC Co.	Raw materials	$6,000.00
DEF Co.	Packaging supplies	1,300.00
GHI Co.	Raw materials	7,200.00

Before preparing financial statements for the year, this $14,500 should be entered in the General Journal as illustrated in Figure 3.4. These entries are then posted in the General Ledger accounts as shown in Figure 3.5. Note that $13,200 is debited to Raw Materials Expense, $1,300 is debited to Packaging Supplies Expense, and the total $14,500 is credited to Accounts Payable. The expense accounts will be cleared after the financial statements are done (see Chapter 12 on Financial Statements). The entries should then be reversed, crediting Raw Materials Expense with $13,200, crediting Packaging Supplies Expense with $1,300, and debiting Accounts Payable with $14,500 (which makes the Accounts Payable balance zero). In the new year the procedure would be the same as for the prior year. When the ABC Company is paid, it will be listed in the Cash Disbursements Journal and debited to Raw Materials Expense.

METHOD 3: ACCRUAL BASIS

If you have a relatively large accounts payable (money you owe to suppliers for goods received but not yet paid for) and want to know where you stand on a month-to-month basis rather than waiting until the end of the year, the straight accrual method may be best for you. This is how it works.

You set up a Purchases Journal as shown in Figure 3.6. You record invoices from suppliers daily as they are received, listing the date of invoice, invoice number, the supplier's name, and the total amount. The dollar amount is written in again under the proper column heading. In some cases one invoice may cover two different expenses such as Office Supplies Expense and Printing Expense. Figure 3.6 illustrates several typical entries.

At the end of the month, you total the columns in your Purchases Journal and post to your General Ledger accounts. The amount from the "total" column will be credited to Accounts Payable as shown in Figure 3.7. The other totals should be debited to the applicable expense accounts. Each item in the "general" column will have to be posted individually to its proper expense account. You

GENERAL JOURNAL   Page 1

	date	description		debit	credit
1	12 31	Raw Materials Ex.		6000	
2		Accounts Payable			6000
3		ABC Co. Inv. 12/16/76			
4					
5		Packaging Supplies Ex.		1300	
6		Accounts Payable			1300
7		DEF. Co. Inv. 12/18/76			
8					
9		Raw Materials Ex.		7200	
10		Accounts Payable			7200
11		GHI Co. Inv. 12/26/76			
12					
13					
14					
15					
16					
17					
18					
19					
20					
21					
22					
23					
24					
25					
26					
27					
28					
29					
30					

FIGURE 3.4 Entries in this General Journal page have been posted to the General Ledger accounts in Figure 3.5.

should check off each item as you post it with a red check mark to avoid duplicate posting. Note that "PJ-3" was written under "folio" on each account in Figure 3.7 to show where the information was obtained.

When you pay invoices, you record the payment as usual in your Cash Disbursements Journal, which should have a column called "Accounts Payable" as shown in Figure 3.8. At the end of the month you total the Accounts Payable column in your Cash Disbursements Journal and debit the amount to Accounts Payable in your General Ledger (see Figure 3.9 for example).

RAW MATERIALS EXPENSE

DATE 19	ITEMS	FOLIO	√	DEBITS	DATE 19	ITEMS	FOLIO	√	CREDITS
12 31	ABC Co. Inv. 12/16	GJ-1		6000					
	GHI Co. Inv. 12/26	GJ-1		7200					

PACKAGING SUPPLIES EXPENSE

DATE 19	ITEMS	FOLIO	√	DEBITS	DATE 19	ITEMS	FOLIO	√	CREDITS
12 31	DEF. Co. Inv. 12/18	GJ-1		1300					

ACCOUNTS PAYABLE

DATE 19	ITEMS	FOLIO	√	DEBITS	DATE 19	ITEMS	FOLIO	√	CREDITS
					12 31	ABC Co. Inv. 12/16	GJ-1		6000
						DEF Co. Inv. 12/18	GJ-1		1300
						GHI Co. Inv. 12/26	GJ-1		7200

FIGURE 3.5 Entries in these General Ledger accounts have been taken from the General Journal page in Figure 3.4.

40

	date	Supplier	Inv.#	total	raw mat.	freight	sm. tool	general	gen acc name
1	2 5	Barnard Supply	3042	520	500	20			
2	2 8	Elco Office Co.	123	150				100	off. Sup. Ex.
3								50	Painting Ex.
4	2 10	Elgin Tool Co.	70005	84		4	80		
5									
6									
7									
8									
9									
10									
11									
12									
13									
14									
15									
16									
17									
18									
19									
20									

FIGURE 3.6 Page from a Purchases Journal showing several entries for purchases. Items are listed in the Purchases Journal as invoices (bills) are received.

ACCOUNTS PAYABLE

DATE 19—		ITEMS	FOLIO	√	DEBITS	DATE 19—		ITEMS	FOLIO	√	CREDITS
						2	28	Feb. Purchases	JT-3		4490

RAW MATERIALS EXPENSE

DATE 19—		ITEMS	FOLIO	√	DEBITS	DATE 19—		ITEMS	FOLIO	√	CREDITS
2	28	Feb. Purchases	JT-3		4090						

FREIGHT EXPENSE

DATE 19—		ITEMS	FOLIO	√	DEBITS	DATE 19—		ITEMS	FOLIO	√	CREDITS
2	28	Feb. Purchases	JT-3		100						

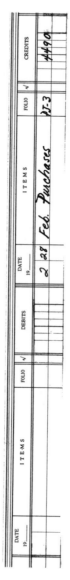

42

SMALL TOOLS EXPENSE

DATE 19__	ITEMS	FOLIO	√	DEBITS	DATE 19__	ITEMS	FOLIO	√	CREDITS
2 28	Feb. Purchases	PJ-3		1 50					

OFFICE SUPPLIES EXPENSE

DATE 19__	ITEMS	FOLIO	√	DEBITS	DATE 19__	ITEMS	FOLIO	√	CREDITS
2 28	Feb. Purchases	PJ-3		1 00					

PRINTING EXPENSE

DATE 19__	ITEMS	FOLIO	√	DEBITS	DATE 19__	ITEMS	FOLIO	√	CREDITS
2 28	Feb. Purchases	PJ-3		50					

FIGURE 3.7 Entries in these General Ledger accounts were taken from page 3 of the Purchases Journal. Note that Accounts Payable is credited and the expense accounts debited.

43

CASH DISBURSEMENTS JOURNAL

Page 5

date	payee	check#	total	accts. payable	salar.	general	gen acct name
3 1	G. Smith	2043	200		200		
3 3	JKL Co.	2044	350	350			
3 3	JMNO Co.	2045	870	870			
3 12	Ecco Bldg. Co.	2046	400			400	Rent Ex.
3 15	PQR Co.	2047	972	972			

FIGURE 3.8 When payments are made to suppliers, list in the Accounts Payable column of Cash Disbursements Journal.

44

ACCOUNTS PAYABLE

DATE 19		I T E M S	FOLIO	√	DEBITS	DATE 19			I T E M S	FOLIO	√	CREDITS
3	31	March Payments	CD-5		4050	*	2	28	Feb. Purchases	PJ-3		4540
		*Prior entry										

FIGURE 3.9 When posting to General Ledger from Cash Disbursements Journal, debit Accounts Payable for payments made to suppliers.

45

ACCOUNTS PAYABLE SUBSIDIARY LEDGER

If you use the strict accrual method of accounting for purchases (method 3), it is a good idea to set up a subsidiary ledger for each supplier you deal with. This allows you to see at a glance how much you owe each one and when payments are due. It gives you a complete record of all business conducted with a supplier. A typical subsidiary ledger should be set up as shown in Figure 3.10.

```
ABC Co.
100 Main St.
Anywhere, USA
```

				①	②	③	④
						credit	
	date	invoice or check#		debit	credit	balance	folio
1	1 31	2054			(a) 540	540	AJ-1
2		2067			(b) 310	850	PJ-1
3	2 28	628		(a) 540			Cd-3
4		3079			(b) 770	1080	PJ-2
5	3 31	3185			250		PJ-3
6		670		(b) 1080		250	Cd-4
7							
8							
9							
10							
11							
12							
13							
14							
15							
16							
17							
18							
19							
20							
21							
22							
23							
24							
25							
26							
27							

FIGURE 3.10 An Accounts Payable subsidiary ledger page for the ABC Company. All invoices and payments are posted from the Purchases Journal and the Cash Disbursements Journal. The credit balance is what is owed the supplier. If there is a debit balance, you put brackets around the amount when you enter it in the "credit balance" column.

At the end of the month you *credit* the entries from your Purchases Journal in the applicable Subsidiary Ledger account; you then *debit* entries from your Cash Disbursements Journal. The difference between credits and debits gives you your credit balance, or the amount you now owe each supplier. The Subsidiary Ledger account in Figure 3.10 shows several months' entries. Note that payments (debits) are keyed to the invoices they cover. Check 628 was a payment for Invoice 2054, so they are both keyed with an (a). Check 670 was a payment for Invoices 2067 and 3079, all keyed with a (b). You should check off entries in the Purchases Journal and Cash Receipts Journal as you post them to the subsidiary ledger in order to avoid duplicate entries.

RETURNS AND REFUNDS

Sometimes you will receive damaged or wrong merchandise, or an order may be short. Whatever the cause, you will want to contact your supplier and request a cash refund or a credit memo which allows you to deduct the amount from your next payment. If your supplier sends a cash refund, you can treat it as any other cash receipt—that is, record the amount in your Cash Receipts Journal as illustrated in Chapter 2, Figure 2.10. At the end of the month you credit the applicable expense account in your General Ledger as illustrated in Chapter 2, Figure 2.11.

If you use method 1 or 2 to record purchases, you should handle credit memos as follows: Deduct the amount of the Credit Memo from your next payment to the supplier. For example, if the invoice you wish to pay is for $150 and the Credit Memo is for $15, you pay the amount of $135. Record the $135 as usual in your Cash Disbursements Journal.

If you are using method 3 for recording purchases, handle Credit Memos as follows: Record them in your Purchases Journal as shown in Figure 3.11. Note that a bracket is put around the amount to indicate it should be subtracted when computing totals. At the end of the month, list the Credit Memo amount as a *debit* in the supplier's Subsidiary Ledger account (see Figure 3.12).

TRIAL BALANCE

Periodically you should take a trial balance of the subsidiary ledger. You make a list of all suppliers, entering the balances from your subsidiary ledger. The total of all balances should match the balance in your Accounts Payable account

PURCHASES JOURNAL

Page 4

18-40B ERASABLE LEDGER	date	supplier	Inv. #	total	raw mat	freight	general	gen-acct name
1	3 20	DAF Co.	CM1004	(13)	(13)			
2								
3								
4								
5								
6								
7								
8								
9								
10								
11								
12								
13								
14								
15								
16								
17								
18								
19								
20								

FIGURE 3.11 Illustration showing how to record a Credit Memo in Purchases Journal. The brackets around the $13 mean it will be debited to subsidiary ledger and subtracted from total purchases credited to Accounts Payable.

48

```
                DEF Co.
                200 Main St.
                Anywhere, USA
```

18-408 EYE EASE LEDGER		date	invoice or check #		① debit	② credit	③ credit balance	④ folio
1		3 31	CM 1004		13			PJ-4
2								
3								
4								
5								
6								
7								
8								
9								
10								
11								
12								
13								
14								
15								
16								
17								
18								
19								
20								

FIGURE 3.12 Subsidiary ledger illustrating the entry of a Credit Memo. Note that the $13 is listed as a debit.

(credits minus debits). Figure 3.13 illustrates a trial balance showing a credit balance that matches the balance in the Accounts Payable account.

TRIAL BALANCE AS OF 6/30/76

Supplier	Credit Balance
ABC COMPANY	$ 230.00
DEF COMPANY	50.00
GHI COMPANY	(15.00)
JKL COMPANY	340.00
MNO COMPANY	—
PQR COMPANY	150.00
STU COMPANY	—
VWX COMPANY	520.00
	$1,275.00

FIGURE 3.13 Trial balance of Accounts Payable and General Ledger Accounts Payable account. (Continued on next page.)

ACCOUNTS PAYABLE

DATE 19—		ITEMS	FOLIO	✓	DEBITS		DATE 19—		ITEMS	FOLIO	✓	CREDITS
1	31	Jan.	Payments	CD-2		670	1	31	Jan.	Purchases	PJ-1	540
2	28	Feb.	"	CD-4		350	2	28	Feb.	"	PJ-2	980
3	30	Mar.	"	CD-6		500	3	30	Mar.	"	PJ-2	1250
4	30	Apr.	"	CD-7		1000	4	30	Apr.	"	PJ-3	1050
5	31	May	"	CD-9		925	5	31	May	"	PJ-4	975
6	30	July	"	CD-11		925	6	30	Jun.	"	PJ-4	950
						4370						5645
												4370
												1275

FIGURE 3.13 (Continued.)

50

If your totals do not match, you should first recheck your figuring, then go back to your Cash Disbursements Journal and make sure that every applicable item is checked off, indicating it has been posted to the subsidiary ledger. You should check especially that refunds were posted properly. The same procedure should be followed with your Purchases Journal. Finally, you should check individual arithmetic on Subsidiary Ledger accounts.

SUMMING UP

A purchase order form should be filled out each time you make a purchase or place an order for supplies, raw materials, finished goods, etc. Keeping these orders filed numerically gives better control. You should also check incoming shipments against them for accuracy.

You will want to use method 1 if you are on the cash basis of accounting for tax purposes. Method 2 or 3 can be used for accrual systems. If you use method 3, you will probably want to set up an Accounts Payable subsidiary ledger. A trial balance of this ledger should be periodically taken and reconciled to your Accounts Payable account.

You should ask for a refund or credit memo when a shipment is short or damaged, and remember to subtract rather than add credit memo amounts on your Purchases Journal and to record them as *debits* on your subsidiary ledger.

4
SALES
AND
ACCOUNTS
RECEIVABLE

This chapter will show you how to invoice your customers, keep a sales journal, write up credit memos, post to general and subsidiary ledgers, and prepare a trial balance of your accounts receivable. The accounts receivable section of this chapter is not applicable to businesses that sell for cash only (do not give credit to their customers).

INVOICES

When you sell services or merchandise to a customer, you will send them a bill or invoice similar to the sample shown in Figure 4.1. The basic purpose of the invoice is to inform the customer when and how goods were shipped; to tell him how much he owes you, and when and under what terms it is due; and to provide a record for you.

Invoices such as the one shown are available at most office supply stores, or can be ordered from the suppliers listed in Chapter 17. It is important to get consecutively numbered invoice forms because that makes it easier to keep track of orders shipped and monies received. These forms are available in carboned sets that provide an original plus as many copies as you may need. Your customers

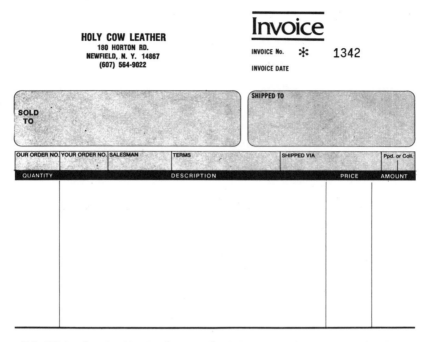

FIGURE 4.1 Standard invoice form, available in consecutively numbered carbon sets and imprinted with company's name and address.

may require two copies of an invoice, in which case you will send them the original and a second copy. You will need two copies for your own files—one to be kept in a consecutively numbered file and another for your customer files. If you have sales representatives, they will need a copy. The last copy of the invoice form, marked "packing slip," can be inserted in the carton of merchandise when it is shipped.

Figure 4.2 is an example of how an invoice might be filled out. The invoice date should be the date merchandise was shipped or picked up by the customer, or the date the service was rendered by your company. Under "sold to," list the name and *billing* address of your customer. Under "shipped to," list the shipping address, if different. Otherwise type in "same."

Under "our order no.," list the number from your own company's order form (see Figure 4.3). Under "your order no.," list the number given on a written order from the customer, if there is one. If a sales representative or company salesperson made the order, list his or her name under "salesman."

Under "terms," list your company's standard payment terms. "Net 30 days" means the invoice must be paid in full within 30 days of the invoice date. "1% 10 net 30" means the customer may deduct one percent of the invoice total

54

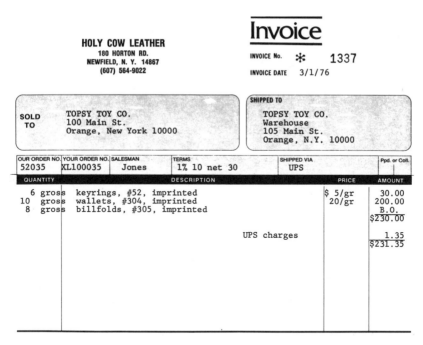

FIGURE 4.2 Completed invoice, ready to send to the customer.

if he pays within 10 days; otherwise the full amount is due within 30 days. "3% 10 EOM" means the customer may deduct three percent from the total and pay the bill by the 10th of the following month. Whatever terms you use should be agreed to in advance by you and your customer.

Under "shipped via," list the carrier (parcel post, United Parcel Service, name of trucking company, etc.) if there was one. If the order was prepaid, check the box marked "Ppd." or type "prepaid" under "terms." If the invoice is to be collected on delivery, check the box marked "coll.," or type "collect" or "C.O.D." under "terms."

The bottom half of the invoice provides space to list the quantity of each item shipped, a description, a unit price, and the total amount. This space is used for listing sales taxes and shipping charges, if any. In the example shown, "B.O." was typed under "amount" for the third item; "B.O." stands for "back order." Although this item was on the customer's order, it was out of stock at the time and was therefore back ordered. Note that no price and amount are listed for this item. It will be invoiced separately when it is shipped. Some customers will not allow back orders and either will want you to wait and ship the whole order at once, or will simply cancel any items you do not have in stock.

HOLY COW LEATHER
113 Nelson Road
Ithaca, New York 14850
Tel. 607 - 273-6678

02123

Order No._____Date_____19____

Name_____

Address_____

Ship To_____

Address_____

WHEN SHIP	HOW SHIP	TERMS	BUYER	SALESMAN	

Rediform
5H 50

FIGURE 4.3 Order forms such as this one are often used by manufacturers and wholesalers, especially when orders are taken by salespeople in the field. A copy of the order is given to the customer so he or she will have a record of what was ordered. The salesperson keeps a copy for his or her records, and the original will be used by you to fill the order and prepare the invoice.

Processing Invoices. Invoices should be typed and sent to customers as soon as possible after orders are shipped—either the same day or at most the following day. Then one copy should be filed in a Sales folder for that month—that is, January Sales, February Sales, etc. These should be filed in numerical sequence so you can keep track of all orders. If a mistake is made in typing an invoice form, a copy should be marked ''void'' and kept in the monthly sales file so you know an order for that number is not missing.

You may want to maintain separate folders for the invoices of each customer in order to see at a glance what you have sold to each account. If you do this, another copy of the invoice is filed in the customer's file. For example, if you send an invoice to the Topsy Toy Company on March 3, you file one copy of the invoice in the March Sales folder and another in the Topsy Toy Company folder.

SALES JOURNAL

A Sales Journal is useful for breaking down total sales by departments or product lines. Figure 4.4 is an example of a page from a typical Sales Journal. Note that invoice numbers are listed consecutively and that some customers have purchased items from several departments on one order.

At the end of each month you should take that month's Sales folder and copy the information from the invoices into your Sales Journal. If weekly information is desired, weekly subtotals are written on the Sales Journal.

If you do not need your total sales broken down into separate departments or product lines, there is no need to keep a Sales Journal. Instead, an adding machine tape of that month's invoices is stapled to the front of the folder. The invoices should be added up twice in order to be sure that the total is correct (this is standard procedure for any computing done in accounting.)

FIGURE 4.4 Sample page from a Sales Journal, with sales recorded for three departments.

SALES JOURNAL   Page 3

	date	customer name	inv. #	Dept. A	Dept. B	Dept. C	invoice total
1	3 25	Mark III Co.	1005	50 -			50 -
2		Topsy Toy Co.	1006		250 -	75 -	325 -
3		Hudson Soap	1007		350 -		350 -
4		Madison Gift	1008	200 -			200 -
5	3 26	Lewis & Son	1009	150 -	35 -	180 -	365 -
6		Mannix Co.	1010		25 -		25 -
7		Solotron Corp.	1011	600 -		500 -	1100 -
8							
9							
10							
11							
12							
13							
14							
15							
16							
17							
18							
19							
20							

CREDIT MEMOS

From time to time it may be necessary to issue a credit memo to a customer because of overcharging, a merchandise return, price adjustments due to damage, and so forth. Figure 4.5 shows an example of a typical credit memo. Note that it is typed on an invoice form, with "CM" typed in front of the invoice number.

Credit memos should be filed in the monthly Sales folder in numerical order with the invoices. When listing them on the Sales Journal, however, brackets should be placed around the amount, which should then be subtracted from the totals. Figure 4.6 illustrates the listing of a credit memo on a Sales Journal. If you do not keep a Sales Journal, be sure to *subtract* credit memos on the adding machine tape.

FIGURE 4.5 Credit Memo issued to a customer for the return of defective merchandise.

Invoice

HOLY COW LEATHER
180 HORTON RD.
NEWFIELD, N. Y. 14867
(607) 564-9022

INVOICE No. ✱ CM 1340

INVOICE DATE   4/15/76

SOLD TO
Lewis & Son
505 Main St.
Charleston, W. Va. 20000

SHIPPED TO

OUR ORDER NO.	YOUR ORDER NO.	SALESMAN	TERMS	SHIPPED VIA	Ppd. or Coll.
		Smith			

QUANTITY	DESCRIPTION	PRICE	AMOUNT
3ea	#405 handbags -- returned - defective, no strap	$8 ea	($24.00)
	CREDIT MEMO		

SALES JOURNAL   Page **4**

	date	customer name	inv. #	① Dept. A	② Dept. B	③ Dept. C	④	⑤ invoice total
1	3 30	Ronson Co.	1062		250 -			250
2		Paper Prod. Corp.	1063	1050 -		300 -		1350
3		Topsy Toy Co.	CM 1064		(24)			(24)
4		Rubber Bubble	1065			840 -		840
5								
6								
7								
8								
9								
10								
11								
12								
13								
14								

FIGURE 4.6 Sample page from a Sales Journal showing a Credit Memo listing.

POSTING SALES TO GENERAL LEDGER

If your sales are strictly on a cash (no credit) basis, sales are recorded directly to the Sales account when the cash is received. To make this entry, you debit Cash and credit Sales. See Figures 2.10 and 2.11 in Chapter 2 for an illustration of the recording of cash sales in the Cash Receipts Journal and the General Ledger.

When selling on a credit basis, however, you not only need to know what your total sales are, but also how much of this total amount has been paid and how much is still outstanding. Therefore you will need an Accounts Receivable account.

Figure 4.7 shows the posting of monthly sales in the Sales and Accounts Receivable accounts. Note that sales are listed on the debit side of the Accounts Receivable and the credit side of the Sales accounts. These monthly figures are taken from the adding machine tapes on the monthly Sales folders. Thus "SF" is listed under "folio" because "SF" stands for "Sales folder."

If you keep a Sales Journal, however, you should set up a Sales account for each department or product line listed in your Journal. You would then post monthly total sales for each department or product line in its appropriate Sales account. See Figure 4.8 for an example of a company with two product lines. Note that sales are broken down into separate Sales accounts, but only one Accounts Receivable account is kept for total sales. "SJ-1, 2, 3," etc., are listed under "folio" to indicate the Sales Journal page the figures were taken from.

SALES

DATE 19__	ITEMS	FOLIO	√	DEBITS	DATE 19__	ITEMS	FOLIO	√	CREDITS
					1 31	Jan. Sales	SF		97 41
					2 28	Feb. Sales	SF		118 42
					3 31	Mar. Sales	SF		147 65

ACCOUNTS RECEIVABLE

DATE 19__	ITEMS	FOLIO	√	DEBITS	DATE 19__	ITEMS	FOLIO	√	CREDITS
1 31	Jan. Sales	SF		97 41					
2 28	Feb. Sales	SF		118 42					
3 31	Mar. Sales	SF		147 65					

FIGURE 4.7 How to post monthly sales to the Sales and Accounts Receivable accounts in the General Ledger.

SALES: PRODUCT A

DATE 19—	ITEMS	FOLIO	√	DEBITS		ITEMS	FOLIO	√	CREDITS
1 30						Jan. Sales	SJ-1		87725
2 28						Feb. Sales	SJ-2		62742
3 31						Mar. Sales	SJ-3		9234

SALES: PRODUCT B

DATE 19—	ITEMS	FOLIO	√	DEBITS		ITEMS	FOLIO	√	CREDITS
1 30						Jan. Sales	SJ-1		10250
2 28						Feb. Sales	SJ-2		12340
3 31						Mar. Sales	SJ-3		11642

ACCOUNTS RECEIVABLE

DATE 19—	ITEMS	FOLIO	√	DEBITS		ITEMS	FOLIO	√	CREDITS
1 30	Jan. Sales	SJ-1		18975					
2 28	Feb. Sales	SJ-2		18582					
3 31	Mar. Sales	SJ-3		20896					

FIGURE 4.8 Posting of monthly sales from a Sales Journal for a company with two product lines.

61

POSTING SALES TO SUBSIDIARY LEDGERS

A subsidiary ledger listing the debits, credits, and outstanding balance for each customer is valuable for providing more control over the credit extended each of your customers. By glancing at the ledger you can tell how often and what amounts they have purchased, the timeliness of their payments, and the present outstanding receivable. When a customer places a new order, you can immediately check their file to see if you should offer them continued credit. By looking through your subsidiary ledger periodically, you can see which customers have become inactive and thereby direct more sales effort toward them. The subsidiary ledger will also be used to prepare an aged trial balance.

Figure 4.9 illustrates a subsidiary ledger with sales posted. You post the sales information on your subsidiary ledger weekly or monthly from the invoices in your monthly Sales folder. The date on the subsidiary ledger sheet is the date of the invoice. The reference number is the invoice number. Sales are listed under debit. Credit memos are listed under credit. The debit balance is the bal-

FIGURE 4.9 A subsidiary ledger sheet.

TOPSY TOY CO.
100 Main Street
Orange, N.Y. 10000   Sales Rep: Marvin Jones

	date	reference #		debit	credit	debit balance	
1	3 / 1	1314		231 35		231 35	
2	3 18	1342		506 -		737 35	
3	3 25	CM 1358			24 -	713 35	
4							
5							
6							
7							
8							
9							
10							
11							
12							
13							
14							
15							
16							
17							
18							
19							
20							

ance owed by the customer. If there is a credit balance due the customer, this would be listed with brackets around it in the debit balance column.

In order to be sure that every invoice is posted to the subsidiary ledger, you should put a check mark in the upper right-hand corner of each invoice as you post it to the subsidiary ledger. In order to be sure not to list an invoice twice, you should post the invoices in numerical order on the subsidiary ledger, just as you file them in the monthly Sales folders.

POSTING CASH RECEIPTS TO THE GENERAL LEDGER

When your credit customers pay their invoices, the checks you receive will be listed under Accounts Receivable in your Cash Receipts Journal (see Chapter 2). Figure 4.10 shows an example of a page in a Cash Receipts Journal listing several accounts receivable items. Note that this page is from the end of the month and totals have been made under the last entries in each column. The total cash received for the month should be posted to the debit side of the Cash account.

FIGURE 4.10 Sample page from a Cash Receipts Journal showing several accounts receivable listings and monthly totals.

CASH RECEIPTS JOURNAL   Page 6

	date	item		total	accounts rec.	general	gen. acct. name	
1	2 26	Rubber Bubble		840 -	840 -			
2		Paper Prod. Co.		1050 -	1050 -			
3		Ronson Co.		250 -	250 -			
4		U. S. Treasury		50 -		50 -	Tax Ex.	
5	2 27	Bank		25 -		25 -	Int. Inc.	
6		Madison Gift		200 -	200 -			
7	2 28	Topsy Toy Co.		325 -	325 -			
8		Lewis & Son		365 -	365 -			
9		Amco Leather		35 -		35 -	Purchases	
10				1425235	141 52 35	100 -		
11								
12								
13								
14								
15								
16								
17								
18								
19								

The Accounts Receivable total is posted to the credit side of the Accounts Receivable account. This posting procedure is illustrated in Figure 4.11. The general items would be posted individually to the credit side of their applicable accounts, as discussed in Chapter 2.

POSTING CASH RECEIPTS TO THE SUBSIDIARY LEDGER

The accounts receivable items on the Cash Receipts Journal (Figure 4.10) should be posted weekly or monthly to your subsidiary ledger. After each item is posted, a red check mark should be placed next to the figure on the Cash Receipts Journal as shown in Figure 4.12. This will insure that all items are posted only once.

Figure 4.13 illustrates a subsidiary ledger with cash receipts posted. The date is taken from the Cash Receipts Journal. The reference number is the page number of the Cash Receipts Journal. The amount received is listed under credit, and subtracted from the debit balance column. The debit balance column shows precisely what the customer owes at all times.

Every record of a payment on the subsidiary ledger should be keyed to the invoices that have been paid. In Figure 4.13, for example, the payment of $231.50 was marked with an A. Since this payment was to cover invoice 314, an A was also placed in front of that invoice amount in the debit column. The next time a payment is made, the letter B will be used to key off the matching invoices, then C, and so on. Sometimes payments may cover two or more invoices, in which case all of them would be keyed with the same letter.

DISCOUNTS

If you allow customers to take discounts for early payment of invoices, they should be recorded as follows: When you receive payment for an invoice, list the invoice amount, not the check amount, as a credit to Accounts Receivable. However, debit the difference to an account called "Discounts" in your General Ledger. You can itemize this under "General" or set up a separate column for it in your Cash Receipts Journal (see Figure 4.14).

If you want to keep track of individual discounts taken by your customers, add a "Discounts" column to your Subsidiary Ledger accounts and when posting payments from your Cash Receipts Journal, list discounts taken as illustrated in Figure 4.15.

When you are preparing financial statements, Discounts will be subtracted from Gross Sales in order to get a Net Sales figure. See Figure 12.18 in Chapter 12 for an example of this.

FIGURE 4.11 Cash and Accounts Receivable accounts showing how to post cash receipts to the General Ledger.

	date	item		total	accounts rec.		general	gen.acct. name
				①	②		③	④
1	2 26	Rubber Bubble		840 –	840 – ✓			
2		Paper Prod. Co.		1050 –	1050 – ✓			
3		Ronson Co.		250 –	250 – ✓			
4		U.S. Treasury		50 –			50 –	Tax Ex.
5	2 27	Bank		25 –			25 –	Int. Inc.
6		Madison Gift		200 –	200 – ✓			
7	2 28	Topsy Toy Co.		325 –	325 – ✓			
8		Lewis & Son		365 –	365 – ✓			
9		Amco Leather		35 –			35 –	Purchases
10				1425235	1415235		100 –	
11								
12								
13								
14								
15								

FIGURE 4.12 Cash Receipts Journal page shown with a check mark after each accounts receivable entry, indicating that it has been posted to the subsidiary ledger.

FIGURE 4.13 Subsidiary ledger sheet illustrating the posting of cash receipts.

TOPSY TOY CO.
100 Main St.
Orange, N.Y.   10000   Sales Rep: Marvin Jones

	date	reference #		debit	credit	debit balance	
				①	②	③	④
1	3 1	1314		(A) 231 35		231 35	
2	3 18	1342		506 –		737 35	
3	3 28	CM 1358			24 –	713 35	
4	4 3	C.R. 4			(A) 231 35	482 –	
5							
6							
7							
8							
9							
10							
11							
12							
13							
14							
15							

CASH RECEIPTS JOURNAL   Page _6_

	date	item		total	accounts rec.	general	gen.acc name
				①	②	③	④
1	2 23	Topsy Toy. Co.		320	325	(5)	Discounts
2							
3							
4							
5							
6							
7							
8							
9							
10							

FIGURE 4.14 Entry in the Cash Receipts Journal showing how to record payment for an invoice on which the customer has taken a discount. The check amount is listed under "total," the invoice amount under "accounts receivable," and the discount in the "general" column. Since this is a Cash Receipts Journal, the "total" column is debited to Cash. All other accounts are credited unless they are in parentheses, in which case they are debited. Since a discount taken by a customer is a debit, it is in parentheses in this example.

FIGURE 4.15 List discounts taken by customers in a "discounts" column in a subsidiary ledger. Note that the $226.72 payment (A) and the discount of $4.63 equal the invoice amount (A) of $231.35.

TOPSY TOY CO
100 Main St.
Orange, N.Y. 10000   Sales Rep: Marvin Jones

	date	reference #		debit	credit	discount	debit balance
				①	②	③	④
1	3 1	1314		(A) 231 35			231 35
2	3 18	1342		506 -			737 35
3	3 28	CM 1358			24 -		713 35
4	4 3	CR-4			(A) 226 72	4 63	482 -
5							
6							
7							
8							
9							
10							
11							
12							
13							
14							
15							

AGED TRIAL BALANCE

Once a month an aged trial balance should be prepared from the information on the subsidiary ledger. Figure 4.16 illustrates a typical trial balance for the month of June, 1976. The company illustrated allows 30-day payment terms to its customers. The "total due" is the debit balance figure from the subsidiary ledger (see the sample subsidiary ledger for this trial balance in Figure 4.17). The "current" figure includes all unpaid invoices billed during the month of June (in this case invoices 10533 and 10589). The 30-day figure includes all unpaid invoices billed in May (30 days past due). The 60-day figure includes all unpaid invoices billed in April. The 90-plus figure includes all unpaid invoices billed prior to April.

The total-due figure for all customers on your trial balance must agree with the total balance of your Accounts Receivable account in the General Ledger. If it does not, first recheck your footing (addition) of both figures. (Note: The Accounts Receivable balance is obtained by adding the debit column and subtracting the credit column for that month.) If your figures still do not match, you should go through your invoices for the month and check to be sure each one was entered on the Accounts Receivable debit column of the General Ledger account and the debit column of the appropriate customer sheet in the subsidiary ledger. If you still cannot find the error you should go through the Cash Receipts Journal and make sure that each Accounts Receivable entry was checked off (meaning it was listed on the subsidiary ledger).

One common error is to enter a credit memo as a regular invoice. All credit memos should be checked to be sure they have been listed properly as credits on subsidiary ledger sheets and subtracted from debit balances.

One way to track down an error is to see if the amount of the error matches a particular invoice or credit memo. If it does not, you can divide by two and see if *this* figure matches.

Once you have found any errors and your totals balance, the next thing to do is to look carefully at past-due amounts on your trial balance. How do these past-due totals for 30, 60, and 90 days or more compare with those of previous months? Which accounts require phone calls, letters, or other dunning procedures? During times of economic stress, you may find credit account payments slowing down to dangerous levels.

The important thing is to detect accounts that might default on their payments and to do everything possible to collect accounts that are past due before bankruptcy or other events seriously reduce the payment capacity of those customers. There are procedures you can take yourself to recover past-due bills, such as phone calls, letters, and legal action. Then there are collection agencies

TRIAL BALANCE: June 30, 1976

		total due	current	30 days	60 days	90+days
	customer name	①	②	③	④	⑤
1	Aamco Corp.	6420	3210	2200	610	400
2	Colins Co.	520	520			
3	Everett Inc.	3928	2678	1250		
4	Fine & Fine	2010	1005	755	250	
5	Lewis & Son	965	620	300	45	
6	Lucky Leather	2845	1525	620	500	200
7	Madison Gift	897	897			
8	Paper Prod. Co.	4500	3050	1450		
9	Ronson Co.	2350	2150	150	50	
10	Rubber Bubble	4000	1200	2050	750	
11	Topsy Toy. Co.	2405	1805	600		
12		30840	18660	9375	2205	600
13						
14						
15						
16						

FIGURE 4.16 Aged trial balance. The first line figures are based on the subsidiary ledger in Figure 4.17.

FIGURE 4.17 Sample subsidiary ledger illustrating the origin of the figures for the first line of the aged trial balance in Figure 4.16.

AAMCO CORP.
800 50th St.
New York, N.Y. 10001   Sales Rep: Martin Spinner

	date	reference #	debit ①	credit ②	debit balance ③
1	2 28				2000
2	3 6	1034	(6)1500		3500
3	3 8	CR-5		(E)2000	1500
4	3 27	10362	400		1900
5	4 5	10401	610		2510
6	5 2	10435	1400		3910
7	5 15	10472	800		4710
8	5 20	CR-8		(6)1500	3210
9	6 7	10533	2100		5310
10	6 28	10589	1110		6420
11					
12					
13					
14					
15					

to assist you in collecting such debts, for a fee or percentage of the amount recovered. Further information on credit and collection procedures is available in several of the books listed in the bibliography at the back of this book.

SUMMING UP

In this chapter you have seen that the subsidiary ledger and the aged trial balance are the tools that provide you with feedback as to the soundness of your credit and collection procedures. Changes in the aged trial balance from month to month can alert you to general changes in your customers' payment habits that may seriously threaten the life and health of your business.

5
RETAIL
STORE
ACCOUNTING

In a retail store it is important to maintain control over the cash and checks flowing in and out of your cash register(s). The daily summary described below is designed to do this. You will also have to take into consideration the value of your inventory in order to compute the cost of goods sold on your income statement. Both the FIFO (first-in, first-out) and gross margin method of valuing inventories are described in this chapter.

CHANGE FUND

It is important to have a change fund that is set at a fixed amount. This amount is kept in the cash register at the end of each day for use the next day. For example, if you have a $50 change fund and cash sales for the day are $250, your total in the cash register will be $300 at the end of the day. You would thus deposit $250 in the bank, leaving the $50 change fund for the next day.

DAILY SUMMARY

At the end of each day, the actual cash on hand is counted and balanced against the total of the receipts recorded for the day. This is done by making a daily summary of sales and cash receipts as shown in Figure 5.1. If you have more than one cash register, make a separate summary for each one and then combine them.

Item 1 on the summary is the cash sales. This is the total day's sales from sales slips or cash register tape. Miscellaneous receipts in item 2 might include refunds from suppliers for overpayments or advertising rebates and allowances. Miscellaneous receipts are itemized on the back of the summary for later entry in your Cash Receipts Journal. Item 3 is the total of items 1 and 2.

To find item 4, you count the coins, bills, and checks in your register. From item 4, you deduct item 5—the change fund—which remains in the cash register. Item 6 is the total cash to be deposited in the bank. This figure should equal item 3—total receipts. If it does, you have reconciled your cash receipts and can stop at this point.

Your daily summary will not always come out right, however. If items 3 and 6 do not agree, you subtract item 7 (which is the same as item 3) from item 6. The difference will be your shortage or overage—item 8 or 9. If you have a

FIGURE 5.1 Daily Summary of sales and cash receipts for a retail store.

DAILY SUMMARY

Cash Receipts

1. Cash sales		$325.00
2. Miscellaneous receipts		20.00
3. Total receipts to be accounted for		$345.00

Cash on Hand

4. Cash in register:		
Coins	24.00	
Bills	260.00	
Checks	107.00	
Total cash in register:		391.00
5. Less: Change fund		50.00
6. Total cash to be deposited		341.00
7. Total receipts to be accounted for		345.00
8. Cash short (item 7 greater than item 6)		4.00
9. Cash over (item 7 less than item 6)		—

Total Sales

10. Cash sales		$325.00

shortage or an overage, recheck your figures carefully. Overages could be caused by neglecting to record or ring up a sale, recording a sale for too small an amount, or giving a customer too little change. Shortages could be caused by recording too large an amount for the sale, giving a customer too much change, or taking money from the cash register without recording it.

As soon as you have finished the daily summary, you should make a deposit at the bank and keep a duplicate deposit slip with the summary as evidence that the deposit was made.

If you have credit customers who buy on open account, your daily summary should include a place to record such transactions. Figure 5.2 is an example of such a daily summary. Note the addition of item 2, "collections on account"; item 12, "charge sales"; and item 13, "total sales."

Recording Returns or Refunds on the Daily Summary. If you use sales checks, a credit sales check marked "cash refund" should be made out when the cash is refunded to the customer. The amount of this refund is deducted from the cash sales figure on the daily summary.

FIGURE 5.2 This Daily Summary has a place to list collections on account (item 2) and charge sales (item 12).

DAILY SUMMARY

Cash Receipts

1. Cash sales		$325.00
2. Collections on account		100.00
3. Miscellaneous receipts		20.00
4. Total receipts to be accounted for		$445.00

Cash on Hand

5. Cash in register:		
Coins	24.00	
Bills	310.00	
Checks	157.00	
Total cash in register:		491.00
6. Less change fund		50.00
7. Total cash deposit		441.00
8. Total receipts to be accounted for		445.00
9. Cash short (item 8 greater than item 7)		4.00
10. Cash over (item 8 less than item 7)		—

Total Sales

11. Cash sales	325.00
12. Charge sales (sales slips No. 151–160)	130.00
13. Total sales	$455.00

If you use a cash register with a return-sales key, you can ring up return sales. Some cash registers subtract return sales directly from sales. In this case the total in the cash register at the end of the day is net sales and can be entered on the daily summary as is. Other cash registers show only the total returned sales, which must be subtracted from the cash register total to get net sales.

Transfer of Daily Summary Totals to Cash Receipts Journal. Daily or weekly, the total cash deposit from the daily summaries is transferred to your Cash Receipts Journal, with miscellaneous receipts itemized in the "general" columns. Figure 5.3 illustrates how information from the daily summary in Figure 5.2 is transferred to a Cash Receipts Journal. Note that the $4 shortage from the Daily Summary is listed in the "general" column to be posted to an account called "shortages/overages." When you post shortages and overages to your General Ledger, you will debit shortages and credit overages. At the end of the year, a net debit balance in this account will become a miscellaneous expense item and a net credit balance will become a miscellaneous income item. At the end of the month these totals will be posted to the General Ledger accounts (see Chapter 2 for detailed description of Cash Receipts Journal and General Ledger).

FIGURE 5.3 Line 7, total cash deposit from the Daily Summary in Figure 5.2, was entered in this Cash Receipts Journal. The $20 miscellaneous receipts and $4 shortage were itemized in the "general" column. Since this is a Cash Receipts Journal, the "total" column is debited to cash. All other accounts are credited unless they are in parentheses, in which case they are debited. Since a cash shortage is a debit, it is in parentheses in this example.

CASH RECEIPTS JOURNAL   Page _3_

	date	item		total ①	accounts rec. ②	cash sales ③	general ④	gen.acct. name ⑤	
1	6 1	CASH RECEIPTS		441 -	100 -	325 -	5 -	Purchases Exp.	
2							15 -	Adv. Exp.	
3							(4)	Shortage/overage	
4									
5									
6									
7									
8									
9									
10									
11									
12									
13									
14									
15									

INCOME STATEMENT

Figure 5.4 illustrates a sample income statement. Note that the cost of goods sold is arrived at by adding beginning inventory to purchases and subtracting ending inventory. The XYZ Company had $20,000 worth of merchandise in inventory at the beginning of the year. Throughout the year they purchased $120,000 worth of additional merchandise. This gave them $140,000 worth of merchandise available for sale. By subtracting the inventory they had left at the end of the year ($25,000), we get the cost of goods sold, or $115,000.

Another way to look at this is to say that the XYZ Company spent a total of $115,000 for the merchandise which they sold for a total of $160,000. In order to compute the cost of goods sold, you must know your total merchandise purchases and the values of your beginning and ending inventories.

Merchandise Purchases. Your yearly total expenditures for merchandise will be recorded in your General Ledger as a Purchases Expense account. Chapter 3 illustrates three methods of recording purchases. As a retail store using an accrual basis of accounting, you will want to use either method 2 or 3.

FIGURE 5.4 Income Statement for a retail store. Cost of goods sold is computed by adding purchases to beginning inventory and subtracting ending inventory.

INCOME STATEMENT FROM 1/1/76 TO 12/31/76

Sales		$160,000
Cost of Goods Sold		
Beginning Inventory	20,000	
Plus Purchases	120,000	
Goods Available for Sale	140,000	
Less Ending Inventory	25,000	
Cost of Goods Sold		115,000
Gross Profit		45,000
Operating Expenses		
Salaries	12,000	
Rent	3,600	
Utilities	900	
Advertising	3,500	
Insurance	500	
Miscellaneous	500	
Total Operating Expenses		21,000
Net Earnings		$ 24,000

Costing Inventories. At the end of each year you must take an actual physical inventory of your merchandise. There are various systems and aids on the market to make this job easier (see Chapter 17). You must then assign a value to this inventory, on a lower-of-cost or market basis. This means you must use whichever is lower—the amount you paid for the item or the amount you can sell it for. For most items your cost will be lower. However, in the case of damaged, obsolete, or out-of-season merchandise, the market value may be lower. You should be sure to separate such stock and assign it a realistic scrap or marked-down value.

For the items valued at cost, FIFO (first-in, first-out) is the most commonly used method of evaluation. This method assumes you sell prior purchases before later purchases of the same item. For example, you purchase product X throughout the year as follows:

50 units Feb. 1 @ $1.00 each
75 units Apr. 1 @ $1.10 each
40 units Aug. 2 @ $1.20 each

At the end of the year you have 50 units in stock. You cost them as follows:

40 units @ $1.20 each = $48.00
10 units @ $1.10 each =   11.00
50 units   = $59.00

The last price you pay for an item will be the value you place on it. When you have more items in stock than you purchased on your last order, you will cost the remainder at the price you paid in your previous order. If you paid the same price for the item all year, it does not matter when you purchased it.

Gross Margin Method of Costing Inventory. The gross margin method of costing inventory is workable if you have a standard (or average) gross margin that is applied to your total inventory or groups of merchandise. In other words, if your cost of goods sold is $X\%$ of sales, you can use this percentage to compute the value of your inventory. The gross margin percentage is calculated as follows:

Total sales: $100,000
Cost of goods sold: −60,000
Gross profit: $ 40,000

$$\frac{\$40,000}{\$100,000} = .40 = 40 \text{ percent gross margin}$$

If your gross margin is consistent, you can take a physical inventory based on the retail price, then multiply by the gross margin and subtract this figure from the retail figure to get the value of your inventory. For example,

Physical inventory @ retail value: $20,000
Gross margin: 40%

$$40\% \times \$20,000 = .4 \times \$20,000 = \$8,000$$
$$\$20,000 - \$8,000 = \$12,000 \text{ inventory value}$$

The reason you might want to use this costing method is its simplicity. If your stock is marked with retail prices, you merely have to add up these prices, rather than look up your cost on each item. If your gross margin varies widely from product to product, however, it may be better to use the standard FIFO method of costing.

The important thing is to use a method that will accurately reflect the value of your inventory. Looking again at the income statement in Figure 5.4, notice that if you value your ending inventory high, it will increase your gross profits for this year and decrease them the following year (this year's ending inventory becomes next year's beginning inventory); and, vice versa, if you undervalue your ending inventory, it will decrease this year's gross profits and increase next year's.

Retail Method for Estimating Inventory Without Taking a Physical Inventory. This procedure allows you to prepare monthly, weekly, or even daily estimates of your inventory. These estimates could be useful for purposes of inventory control and formulating purchasing policy. The method is as follows:

	Cost	Retail
Inventory at beginning of period	$ 5,000	$ 7,500
Purchases during the period	55,000	92,500
Totals	$60,000	$100,000

(Ratio of cost to retail—60%—60,000:100,000)

Sales for period	$ 90,000
Inventory at retail ($100,000–$90,000)	$ 10,000

Inventory computation—60% of $10,000 = $6,000 estimated inventory at cost

Inventory Control. In a retail store it is important to know what you have in stock, how fast it is moving, and when to reorder. In some small shops you can reorder after merely checking your shelves visually. However, a perpetual inventory system may be necessary. Figure 5.5 illustrates a typical perpetual inventory sheet for a single product. A sheet is needed for each product or product line carried.

Note that the perpetual inventory sheet has a place to record sales of the merchandise, shipments received, and the balance in stock. Columns are also provided to list goods ordered and the price paid for them.

PERPETUAL INVENTORY RECORD

Product Name _____ Code _____ Page *1*

date	unit sales	units on order	shipments rec'd	price	balance in stock
1/15		150		2 ea.	0
2/10			150	300	150
3/1	35				115
4/1	60				55
4/2		200		2.10 ea	55
5/1	45				10
5/3			200		210

FIGURE 5.5 Perpetual inventory record. Set it up to give the necessary information needed to make re-order decisions. Periodically (at least once a year) match perpetual inventory balance with a physical inventory.

Perpetual inventory records are useful for reorder decisions. They indicate how fast an item is moving, time lapse between order placement and receipt of goods, and current prices paid. You may also want to total your perpetual inventory records to get ending inventory figures for monthly income statements. At least once a year, however, a physical inventory should be taken. By matching your physical and perpetual inventory records, you will find errors, indications of theft, and other losses.

SUMMING UP

You should keep a standard change fund and record daily receipts of cash and checks from your register in a daily summary. This information is transferred to your Cash Receipts Journal on a daily or weekly basis. See Chapter 2 for posting to the General Ledger.

In a retail store, the value of your ending inventory will affect the gross profits on your income statement. The Internal Revenue Service requires that you cost this inventory at the lower-of-cost or market value. To do this, you use either the FIFO * or gross margin costing method. You should also be sure not to overvalue goods that must be sold at a loss due to damage, style changes, or other factors.

Keeping a perpetual inventory is useful for reordering decisions. It can also be used for valuing inventory on monthly income statements in place of taking a physical inventory The retail method of estimating inventory values without taking a physical inventory can also be used for monthly or weekly financial statements. At least once a year, however, you should take a physical inventory and match it against the perpetual records.

* There is another method, LIFO (last-in, first-out), which has been omitted because of its complexity.

6
ACCOUNTING
FOR
MANUFACTURING
EXPENSES

As a manufacturer, you will want to separate your manufacturing expenses from your sales and administrative expenses. This is necessary in order for you to calculate the cost of making your products, that is, the cost of goods sold. You will also have to keep track of an inventory, which will be made up at any one time of raw materials, work in process, and finished goods. In this chapter we will discuss how to record your manufacturing expenses, compute the cost of goods sold, place a value on your physical inventory, and keep a perpetual inventory record.

INCOME STATEMENT

A sample income statement for a manufacturing company is shown in Figure 6.1. Note that the cost of goods sold is arrived at by adding the beginning inventory (the inventory at the beginning of the year) to purchases, labor, and manufacturing overhead and subtracting the ending inventory. Purchases include all raw materials used to manufacture the products. Labor is the direct labor costs (salaries to employees who make the products, not salespeople, clerical help, etc.) including salaries, payroll taxes, and benefits. Manufacturing overhead is a

INCOME STATEMENT FROM 1/1/76 TO 12/31/76

Sales		$300,000
Cost of Goods Sold		
Beginning Inventory	50,000	
Purchases	75,000	
Labor	125,000	
Manufacturing Overhead	25,000	
	275,000	
Less Ending Inventory	75,000	
Cost of Goods Sold		200,000
Gross Profit		100,000
Sales and Administrative Expenses		
Salaries	30,000	
Rent	2,500	
Utilities	500	
Office Supplies	300	
Printing Supplies	1,000	
Promotion Expenses	15,000	
Insurance	500	
Miscellaneous	200	
Sales and Administrative Expenses		50,000
Net Earnings		$ 50,000

FIGURE 6.1 Income Statement for a manufacturing company showing how cost of goods sold is figured.

percentage of total rent, utilities, etc., which is allocated to the manufacturing end of the business. For example, if five-sixths of your building is used for manufacturing and one-sixth for office space, you would allocate five-sixths of your rent expense to manufacturing overhead.

Labor Costs. In order to separate manufacturing labor costs from sales and administrative labor costs, you should maintain separate salary expense accounts in your General Ledger as shown in Figure 6.2. Salaries for sales people, office clerks, etc., would be posted to sales and administrative salaries expenses. Salaries for laborers, foremen, and manufacturing supervisors would be posted to manufacturing labor expenses. If you have a large number of employees, you may wish to have two columns in your Cash Disbursements Journal for listing salary expenses, as shown in Figure 6.3.

If you have an employee whose time is divided between manufacturing and administrative or sales functions (for example, a general manager), you can

MANUFACTURING SALARIES EXPENSE

DATE 19__	ITEMS	FOLIO	√	DEBITS	DATE 19__	ITEMS	FOLIO	√	CREDITS
3 31	March Salaries	CD-5		1512 -					

SALES & ADMINISTRATIVE SALARIES EXPENSE

DATE 19__	ITEMS	FOLIO	√	DEBITS	DATE 19__	ITEMS	FOLIO	√	CREDITS
3 31	March Salaries	CD-5		824					

FIGURE 6.2 Separate labor expenses by keeping a separate account for manufacturing salaries and one for sales and administrative salaries, as shown here.

CASH DISBURSEMENTS JOURNAL   Page 5

	date	payee	check#	total	mfg.sal	Ad.sal	raw materials	mfg. suppls.	general	gen.acct name
1	3/1	H. Smith	4052	225-	225-					
2		R. Boland	4053	210-	210-					
3		S. Leland	4054	320-	170-	150-				
4		R. Beecher	4055	180-		180-				
5										
6										
7										
8										
9										
10										
11										
12										
13										
14										
15										
16										
17										
18										
19										
20										

FIGURE 6.3 Example of separate columns in Cash Disbursements Journal for manufacturing salaries and sales and administrative salaries.

84

handle the division in either of two ways. If you have a general manager who devotes 40 percent of his time to manufacturing and 60 percent to administration and sales, you could list his whole salary under administration and sales expenses. Then at the end of the year when you prepare to make up financial statements, you credit sales and administrative salary expenses with 40 percent of his yearly salary and debit manufacturing labor expenses with the same amount. Another solution would be to allocate 40 percent of his salary to manufacturing expenses throughout the year.

Manufacturing Overhead. Throughout the year you keep track of rent, utilities, insurance, supplies, etc., in the usual manner. Then before preparing your financial statements, you must decide what percentage of these costs should be allocated to manufacturing overhead. You may base this on the amount of space that is used for manufacturing, or use some other method that you feel more accurately reflects the overhead used. For example, if there are two toilets in the plant and one in the office, you can allocate two-thirds of the cost of toilet supplies to manufacturing overhead. Or you may wish to come up with one fraction or percentage to apply to the total amount of overhead expenses.

Purchases. Your purchases of raw materials and the supplies used in manufacturing are recorded separately from purchases for sales or administrative uses. Chapter 3 shows several methods for recording purchases depending on whether you are on a cash or accrual basis of accounting. Since you are a manufacturer, you will want to use either method 2 or 3. You must keep separate accounts in your General Ledger for manufacturing purchases and administrative and sales purchases. Figure 6.4 illustrates two supplies expense accounts set up to separate supplies used in manufacturing from supplies used in administration and sales.

Inventory. At the end of the year a physical inventory must be taken. Then it is costed and this figure is listed as "ending inventory" on the income statement (see Figure 6.1). The following year this amount will be listed as "beginning inventory." For a company in its first year of operation, the beginning inventory figure would be zero.

In a manufacturing company the physical inventory at any one time usually consists of some finished goods, some work in process, and some raw materials. When you take your physical inventory, you must count and label goods in all three categories. You will then be ready to cost or compute the value of this inventory.

Raw Materials. The Internal Revenue Service offers several acceptable methods of costing inventories. The one most commonly used by small manufacturing

MANUFACTURING SUPPLIES EXPENSE

DATE 19—	ITEMS	FOLIO	√	DEBITS		DATE 19—	ITEMS	FOLIO	√	CREDITS
3 3	Elcon Supply Inc.	co-6		180	—					
3 18	Clean Case Co.	co-8		52	—					

SALES & ADMINISTRATIVE SUPPLIES EXPENSE

DATE 19—	ITEMS	FOLIO	√	DEBITS		DATE 19—	ITEMS	FOLIO	√	CREDITS
3 4	Office Sup. Co.	co-6		34	—					
3 10	Paper Prod. Co.	co-7		56	—					

FIGURE 6.4 Manufacturing supplies expenses recorded separately from sales and administrative supplies expense in two General Ledger accounts.

companies is FIFO * (first-in, first-out). This method assumes that materials purchased earlier are used before the same kind of materials purchased later in the year. An example of how it works follows:

Jan.	purchase of 1,000 No. 5 rods at 5¢ ea.	$ 50
Mar.	purchase of 2,000 No. 5 rods at 6¢ ea.	120
Jun.	purchase of 2,500 No. 5 rods at 6¢ ea.	150
Nov.	purchase of 3,000 No. 5 rods at 7¢ ea.	210

On December 31 you have 1,000 No. 5 rods in stock. Their value is 7¢ × 1,000 or $70.00. If you had 4,000 No. 5 rods in stock on December 31, they would be valued as follows:

3,000 would be worth 7¢ ea.	$210
1,000 would be worth 6¢ ea.	60
Total value of 4,000 rods:	$270

The above example illustrates that FIFO assumes you used up the rods purchased in January and March before you used the ones purchased in June and November. This means that you cost raw materials at the latest prices paid for them. If prices went down instead of up as in our example, the rods would be costed at these new lower prices.

So your first step in computing the value of your ending inventory is to cost out all raw materials in stock using the FIFO method shown above. However, no goods should be costed at higher than their market value. Therefore, if you have outdated or spoiled raw materials in stock, they should be priced at their salvage value, not what you paid for them.

Finished Goods. Finished goods should be valued at what it costs you to make them, unless their market value is lower than this figure, as it might be for obsolete goods or products that have gone out of style and will have to be sold at a loss. In this instance you use their lowest value or worth. Normally, however, you value finished goods at what it costs you to make them. This means you have to compute the raw materials, labor, and manufacturing overhead expenses it costs to produce them.

You may have already established what it costs you to make your products. You may, for example, work on an overall gross margin for each product line. You know that you sell Product A for $40, leaving you a gross margin of $10, or 25 percent. If your average gross margin is 25 percent on all products, you could compute the value of finished goods by taking 75 percent of their total sale price.

* There is another method, LIFO (last-in, first-out), which was not discussed due to its complexity.

Work in Process. To estimate the value of work in process, you take a percentage of the finished-goods value of the items. For example, if a finished Product A is worth $6.00, one that is half finished will be worth $3.00. The closer to completion, the closer to full value the work in process will be worth. A straight fraction may not always be accurate, however. Suppose $50 worth of raw materials were put into a product that was still only half finished in terms of labor. It would be worth $50 plus half the labor costs, plus half the overhead costs.

It is difficult to give any one method for valuing inventories in manufacturing firms because of the variations in each company. As a general guideline, the larger the ending inventory is in comparison to cost of goods sold, the more accurately it should be costed.

Looking again at Figure 6.1, you will notice that the higher the value given to ending inventory, the higher the gross profit margin. If you overvalue the worth of your ending inventory, you will show a higher profit that year and consequently a lower profit margin the following year (because the first year's ending inventory becomes the next year's beginning inventory); and, vice versa, if you undervalue your inventory, you will show a lower profit the first year and a higher one the next year.

COSTING INVENTORY BY ESTIMATING VALUE OF FINISHED GOODS AND WORK IN PROCESS *

This method has been used successfully by small manufacturers to compute the value of their inventories. It is based on the ratio of total labor and overhead expenses to total materials to which labor has been applied. In addition, you must assign a completion factor (percentage) to work in process and have costed separately the materials in (1) raw materials, (2) work in process, and (3) finished goods inventories.

To cost your inventory using this method, do the following: *In first year of operations* (assuming no beginning inventory) you will need the following figures from your end-of-the-year trial balance (see Chapter 12): total manufacturing labor expense; total manufacturing overhead expense; and total manufacturing purchases. For this example, we'll assume:

Total year manufacturing expense:	$100,000
Total year manufacturing overhead:	200,000
Total year manufacturing purchases:	700,000

* This method is not recommended if a product mix is not homogeneous, that is, if there is a wide variation in the proportion of materials, labor, and overhead costs of the products. For example, cloth and finished clothing are not homogeneous because there is a larger percentage of labor in the total cost of manufacturing finished clothing than cloth.

Use the FIFO method (see above) to cost your raw materials inventory. Using this same method, cost the *materials* in work in process and finished goods inventories. For our example, we'll assume:

Raw materials inventory:	$ 60,000
Materials in work in process:	30,000
Materials in finished goods:	40,000
Total materials in inventory:	$130,000

Adjust the total year purchases figure by subtracting your raw materials inventory:

$$\$700,000 - \$60,000 = \$640,000 \text{ adjusted purchases}$$

This adjusted purchases figure more accurately reflects the value of all materials to which labor has been applied throughout the year. Add labor to overhead expenses and divide by adjusted purchases:

$$\$100,000 + \$200,000 = \$300,000 \div \$640,000 = .468 =$$
47 percent labor and overhead: purchases ratio

Next, estimate the average percentage completion of work in process. In other words, if work in process is spread out evenly—from one percent to 99 percent completed—you may want to use a 50 percent completion factor. If more goods are nearer to completion, you may feel 60 percent or 75 percent would be more accurate. In any case, pick one average percentage to use as your completion factor. In our example we'll use 75 percent.

To compute the labor and overhead costs of finished-goods inventory, multiply the materials cost times the labor and overhead: purchases ratio:

$$\$40,000 \times .47 = \$18,800 \text{ labor and overhead cost of finished goods}$$

To compute the labor and overhead costs of work in process, you must first multiply by the completion factor (75 percent), then by the labor and overhead: purchases ratio:

$$\$30,000 \times 75 \text{ percent} \times .47 = \$10,575 \text{ labor and overhead cost of work in process}$$

By adding these labor and overhead costs to total materials costs, you get the total cost of your inventory:

Total materials in inventory:	$130,000
Labor and overhead cost of finished goods:	18,800
Labor and overhead cost of work in process:	10,575
	$159,375 total inventory

The following is a chart illustrating the process:

	Col. 1	Col. 2	Col. 3	Col. 4	Col. 5	Col. 6
	Materials cost at FIFO	Completion factor	Col. 1 × Col. 2	Labor and overhead: purchases ratio	Col. 4 × Col. 3	Col. 1 + Col. 5
Raw materials	60,000	0	0	.47	0	60,000
Work in process	30,000	.75	22,500	.47	10,575	40,575
Finished goods	40,000	1.00	40,000	.47	18,800	58,800
Total	130,000		62,500		29,375	159,375

Note that no labor and overhead are assigned to the raw materials, with a completion factor of zero. Finished goods have a 100 percent completion factor.

For Second and Succeeding Years of Operation. You cannot assume that the ratio of labor and overhead costs to purchases will remain the same from year to year. You may have improved the efficiency of your operation and therefore be using less labor or overhead, or both, for each dollar of purchases; or your product mix may be changed so that now you are producing items that use more labor or overhead costs, or both, per purchases dollar.

To adjust the purchases figure in the second year, you must add the beginning year's raw-materials inventory and subtract the ending raw-materials inventory. This will give you an adjusted purchases figure that accurately reflects the value of all materials to which labor has been applied throughout the year (beginning raw-materials inventory must be added because these materials were used up during the year).

To begin, first price out (using FIFO) your raw materials and materials used in work-in-process and finished goods inventories, as you did the prior year. For our example, let us assume the following:

	Col. 1	Col. 2	Col. 3	Col. 4	Col. 5	Col. 6
	Materials cost at FIFO	Completion factor	Col. 1 × Col. 2	Labor and overhead: purchases ratio	Col. 4 × Col. 3	Col. 1 + Col. 5
Raw materials	70,000	0	0			
Work in process	35,000	.75	26,250			
Finished goods	50,000	1.00	50,000			
Total	155,000		76,250			

From the trial balance, take the total manufacturing labor, overhead, and purchases figures as follows:

Total manufacturing labor:	$150,000
Total manufacturing overhead:	$200,000
Total manufacturing purchases:	$900,000

To adjust the purchases figure, add the beginning raw-materials inventory and subtract the ending raw-materials inventory as follows:

Purchases:	$900,000	
Plus raw materials, beginning inventory:	60,000	(last year's ending
	$960,000	inventory)
Less raw materials, ending inventory	70,000	
	$890,000	adjusted purchases

To compute labor and overhead: purchases ratio, add labor to overhead and divide by adjusted purchases as follows:

$$\$150,000 + \$200,000 = \$350,000 \div \$890,000 = .393 = 39 \text{ percent}$$

Complete the computation for this second year as you did the first year as follows:

	Col. 1	Col. 2	Col. 3	Col. 4	Col. 5	Col. 6
	Materials cost at FIFO	Completion factor	Col. 1 × Col. 2	Labor and overhead: purchases ratio	Col. 4 × Col. 3	Col. 1 + Col. 5
Raw materials	70,000	0	0	.39	0	70,000
Work in process	35,000	.75	26,250	.39	10,238	45,238
Finished goods	50,000	1.00	50,000	.39	19,500	69,500
Total	155,000		76,250		29,738	184,738

PERPETUAL INVENTORY RECORDS

You may wish to keep a perpetual inventory of raw materials for reordering purposes. The setup shown in Figure 6.5 gives you information at a glance as to when you purchased a particular material, its price, and a current balance of quantity in stock. You should set up an inventory sheet for each kind of raw material, small tools, supplies, etc., which you regularly purchase.

INVENTORY RECORD

MATERIAL: Rods, #5   Page _1_

	date	units purchased		price	units used	balance
1	1 4	3,000		05		3000
2	18				500	2500
3	25				1500	1000
4	2 16	2,000		06		3000
5						
6						
7						
8						
9						
10						
11						
12						
13						
14						
15						
16						
17						
18						
19						
20						

FIGURE 6.5 Perpetual inventory record for raw materials.

Periodically (at least once a year) you should take a physical inventory of your raw materials to check the accuracy of your perpetual inventory records. Comparing actual physical inventory against perpetual records is a good way to see if you are suffering losses due to theft. You may find, however, that differences between perpetual records and the physical count are due to clerical errors.

SUMMING UP

The most important thing in manufacturing accounting is to ascertain accurately the cost of goods sold. With this knowledge you will be able to confirm profit expectations, control pricing procedures, and make informed management decisions. This means you must separate manufacturing expenses from sales and administrative expenses. Doing so will inform you as to which costs are incurred in making your products, selling your products, and administering your business.

7
ACCOUNTING
FOR
FIXED
ASSETS

Your company's assets can be broken down into two categories: current and fixed. Current assets include cash, inventories, and other items such as accounts receivable which will be converted to cash within a short period (usually one year). Prepaid insurance and prepaid expenses are also current assets because if they had not been prepaid, cash would be used within the year to pay for them.

Fixed assets include land, buildings, vehicles, and equipment owned by the company that will be used over a long period of time. The Internal Revenue Service requires that such assets * be capitalized over their useful lifetime rather than expensed as you would other business expenditures. If you buy small tools that will be replaced within the year, this would be an expense. You would charge the whole cost of the tools as a business expense in the year you purchased them. If you buy a machine that will be used for 10 years, however, you cannot take the whole cost of this machine as an expense in the year you purchased it. Rather, you must spread the total cost over the 10-year period, claiming a part of it as an expense during each of those years.

You should establish a capitalization policy for your business and stick to it.

---

* Land is not depreciated or charged as an expense. It remains on your balance sheet as an asset at its original cost.

For example, you may decide to capitalize everything that has a useful life of two or more years and cost $200 or more. The exact policy will depend on the size of your business, but you must be careful not to overstep the limits placed by the Internal Revenue Service. By *not* capitalizing an asset, you reduce your income taxes in the year in which you purchased it.

Generally, there is no point in capitalizing items that you buy every year. For example, if you buy approximately the same number of dies each year, there is no point in capitalizing them. In addition to the item's cost, you should consider the useful life it will have for your business. If an item cost $300, but becomes outmoded within a year, there is no point in capitalizing it because it will not be useful after the first year.

PURCHASE OF FIXED ASSETS

When you purchase fixed assets such as vehicles or machinery and equipment, you make an entry on your Cash Disbursements Journal as shown in Figure 7.1. This entry will be posted to the debit side of a Fixed Assets account in your General Ledger (see Figure 7.2).

The purchase of fixed assets should also be recorded in a schedule as illustrated in Figure 7.3. Note that there is a place to list the cost of the asset; its estimated useful life (ask the Internal Revenue Service for its guidelines on useful life for various types of equipment); the depreciation method you are using (see below); and the amount of depreciation taken each year. Every time you purchase a fixed asset, you add it to this schedule. When you compute depreciation at the end of the year, you will list it in the applicable column for that year. The fixed asset purchases on this schedule should agree with the acquisitions in your Fixed Asset account in the General Ledger.

DEPRECIATION METHODS

Depreciation is a way of accounting for the fact that a fixed asset has a useful life of several years. Each year it depreciates, or becomes worth less than its original value, because its useful life is now a year shorter. To look at it simply, if a machine costs $10,000 and has a useful life of 10 years, each year it depreciates $1,000 in value. If the machine has no scrap value and a life of 10 years, you could claim $1,000 depreciation expense for this machine for each of those 10 years. This is the straight-line method of depreciation.

If this same machine could be sold at the end of the 10 years for $500, this

CASH DISBURSEMENTS JOURNAL

Page 2

	date	payee	check#	total	accounts payable	salaries	supplies	general	gen. acct. name
1	2/4	Allied Mach. Corp.	1278	10000-				10000-	Fixed Assets
2									
3									
4									
5									
6									
7									
8									
9									
10									
11									
12									
13									
14									
15									
16									
17									
18									
19									
20									

FIGURE 7.1 Cash Disbursements Journal showing the entry of a fixed asset purchase.

FIXED ASSETS

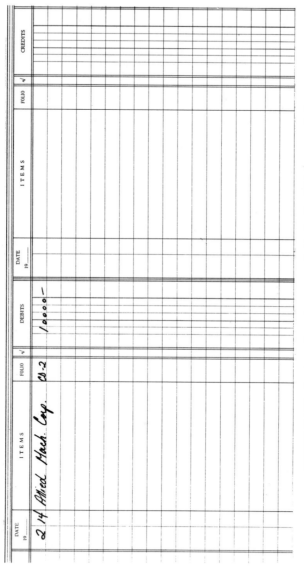

FIGURE 7.2 The fixed asset purchase recorded in the Cash Disbursements Journal in Figure 7.1 posted to the debit side of the Fixed Assets General Ledger account.

salvage value would have to be deducted from the $10,000 before dividing by 10, as follows:

$$\$10,000 - \$500 = \$9,500 \div 10 = \$950 \text{ depreciation expense}$$
$$\text{per year}$$

The Internal Revenue Service allows several depreciation methods to be used. You may never charge more depreciation expense than the asset cost. For example, if after 10 years you found the above machine would last another three years, you could not continue to take $950 depreciation expense each of those years.

Declining-Balance Method. The declining-balance method of depreciation allows you to charge a larger depreciation expense in the first years after purchase of a fixed asset. By using the declining-balance method, your income taxes will be lower during these years than with the straight-line method. Consequently, you'll have less depreciation expense and higher income taxes in later years.

For *new* equipment with minimum useful life of three years:

Year 1:   Take a percentage *double* the straight-line method
Each remaining year: Take same percentage of remainder (book value)

EXAMPLE. A new $10,000 machine is purchased with a useful life of 10 years. It would be depreciated at 10 percent per year using straight line (see above). Under declining balance, you would use double, or 20 percent.

> Year 1: 20 percent of $10,000 = $2,000
> Year 2: 20 percent of $8,000 ($10,000 − $2,000) = $1,600
> Year 3: 20 percent of $6,400 ($8,000 − $1,600) = $1,280
> Year 4: 20 percent of $5,120 ($6,400 − $1,280) = $1,024
> And so on

For *used* equipment with minimum useful life of three years:

Year 1:   Take a percentage 1½ times the straight-line method
Each remaining year: Take same percentage of book value

EXAMPLE. A used $10,000 machine is purchased with a useful life of 10 years. It would be depreciated at 10 percent per year using straight line. Under declining balance, you would use 1½ times, or 15 percent.

> Year 1: 15 percent of $10,000 = $1,500
> Year 2: 15 percent of $8,500 ($10,000 − $1,500) = $1,275
> Year 3: 15 percent of $7,225 ($8,500 − $1,275) = $1,083.75
> And so on

DATE	VENDOR	COST	ESTIMATED Useful LIFE	SALVAGE VALUE & DEP. METHOD	1ST YR.	2nd YR.	3rd
	Machinery & Equipment						
2 14	Allied Mach. Corp.	10,000 -	10 yrs.	db-20%			
3 17	Hunter Equip. Co.	3,000 -	5 yrs.	db-15%			
	VEHICLES						
1 9	GM Sales	6,000 -	6 yrs.	S.l.$400			

FIGURE 7.3 How to set up a Fixed Assets Purchases Schedule.

The salvage value is not considered in this method, except that you may not depreciate beyond the salvage value. You may change from the declining-balance to the straight-line method at any time during the useful life of the asset, but after that you may not change back to the declining-balance method without permission from the Internal Revenue Service.

Additional First-Year Depreciation. The Internal Revenue Service allows you to take an additional 20 percent depreciation in the first year as long as certain criteria are met. The following covers the basic points:

1. You must take this additional deduction in the year you acquire the property.
2. Property may be new or used, having a useful life of at least six years.
3. The cost of the property is limited to $10,000 on a separate return, and $20,000 on a joint return (corporations are limited to $10,000).
4. See Internal Revenue Publication 334 for additional detailed requirements.

Yr.	4th Yr	5th Yr	6th Yr	7th Yr	8th Yr	9th Yr	10th Yr.	

EXAMPLE. On January 4, 1977, you purchase a $15,000 machine. It has a useful life of 10 years and a salvage value of $500.

Additional first-year depreciation:
  ($15,000 limited to $10,000)   20 percent of $10,000 = $2,000
Regular straight-line depreciation:
  ($15,000 less the $2,000 less $500) 10 percent of $12,500 = $1,250
        Total depreciation for year $3,250

Recording Depreciation Expenses. When you have computed the depreciation on a fixed asset at the end of the year, you list the depreciation on your schedule as shown in Figure 7.4. Note that assets purchased during the year are depreciated at an appropriate fraction for the first year, that is, if you bought the asset in June, you would depreciate it for six months, or half the normal amount. To avoid having to compute depreciation for odd fractions of a year, the Internal Revenue Service allows you to use an average, charging one-half year's depreciation at the end of the year for all assets purchased within that year, no matter in what month they were purchased.

99

Date	Vendor	Cost	Estimate Useful Life	Dep. Method & Salvage Value	1st Yr	2nd Yr
	MACHINERY & EQUIPMENT					
		10000 –	10 yrs	db – 20%	2000 –	
1 3	Allied Mach. Co.	3000 –	5 yrs	Sl. $300	270 –	
6 2	Hunter Equip. Co.					
	VEHICLES					
1 9	GM Sales	6000 –	8 yrs	Sl. $400	700 –	

FIGURE 7.4 First-year depreciation computed and entered in Fixed Assets Purchases Schedule. In the first entry the declining balance method was used. The 20 percent (double the straight line of one tenth or 10 percent) of $10,000 is $2,000. In the second entry, the straight-line method was used and the machine has a salvage value of $300. The 20 percent (one fifth) of $2,700 is $540.00. Since the machine was purchased in June, only one-half year's depreciation can be taken the first year (½ × $540 = $270). In the third entry, the straight-line method was used and the vehicle has a salvage value of $400 (⅛ × $5,600 = $700).

100

3rd yr.	4th yr.	5th yr.	6th yr.	7th yr.	8th yr.	9th yr.	10th yr.	

Next, you make an entry in your General Journal as shown in Figure 7.5. The depreciation is then posted in the General Ledger as a debit to Depreciation Expense and a credit to Accumulated Depreciation (see Figure 7.6). The total depreciation expense for the year will appear on your income statement as illustrated in Figure 7.7. The total accumulated depreciation will be listed on your balance sheet under Fixed Assets as shown in Figure 7.8.

101

GENERAL JOURNAL   Page _3_

	date	item	debit	credit
1	12 31	Depreciation Expense	2970 -	
2		Accumulated Depreciation		2970 -
3		1976 Depreciation		
4				
5				
6				
7				
8				
9				
10				
11				
12				
13				
14				
15				
16				
17				
18				
19				
20				
21				
22				
23				
24				
25				
26				
27				
28				
29				
30				

FIGURE 7.5 Depreciation, after computation, recorded in the General Journal.

After your financial statements are prepared, the Depreciation Expense account will be cleared for the next year, as are all income and expense accounts. However, the Fixed Assets and Accumulated Depreciation accounts will continue to increase as equipment is purchased and depreciation is taken in the future. The balance in the Fixed Asset account will always be the total cost of equipment on hand. The balance in the Accumulated Depreciation account will always be the total depreciation taken on the assets in the Fixed Assets account. Only when you sell or scrap the asset will it be written off in these two accounts. We see how this is done below.

102

DEPRECIATION EXPENSE

DATE 19___	ITEMS	FOLIO	√	DEBITS
12 31 1976	Depreciation	61-3		2970 —

DATE 19___	ITEMS	FOLIO	√	CREDITS

ACCUMULATED DEPRECIATION

DATE 19___	ITEMS	FOLIO	√	DEBITS

DATE 19___	ITEMS	FOLIO	√	CREDITS
12 31 1976	Depreciation	61-3		2970 —

FIGURE 7.6 Posting of depreciation as a debit to Depreciation Expense and a credit to Accumulated Depreciation.

INCOME STATEMENT FROM 1/1/76 TO 12/31/76

Sales		$100,000
Operating Expenses		
Rent	10,000	
Salaries	40,000	
Supplies	5,000	
Insurance	1,000	
Promotion	10,000	
Depreciation Expense	2,970 *	
Utilities	1,000	
Miscellaneous	5,000	
Total Operating Expenses		74,970
Income		$ 25,030
Retained Earnings, Beginning Year:		5,000
Retained Earnings, End of Year:		$ 30,030

* This is the total depreciation expense for the year

FIGURE 7.7 Income Statement showing Depreciation Expense listed as an operating expense.

Selling a Fixed Asset at Salvage Value. Suppose at the end of the tenth year, you sell the $10,000 machine discussed above for $500 after having charged a total depreciation of $9,500 over the 10-year period. You would list the $500 in your Cash Receipts Journal and it would be posted as a debit to Cash and a credit to Fixed Assets account.

You no longer have the machine, however, so you would enter the $9,500 in your General Journal as a debit to Accumulated Depreciation and a credit to Fixed Assets as shown in Figure 7.9. When this entry is posted to the Accumulated Depreciation and Fixed Assets accounts, the new balances will reflect a deduction of the $9,500 machine. This means it will no longer appear on your balance sheet as part of Fixed Assets or Accumulated Depreciation. Here is a summary of the procedure:

(a) Machine is purchased.
(b) 10 years of depreciation on straight-line method: $10 \times \$950 = \$9,500$.
(c) Machine is sold at salvage value ($500).
(d) Machine is written off books.

BALANCE SHEET AS OF 12/31/76

Current Assets			*Liabilities*		
Cash		$20,000	Loans Payable		$ 3,500
Prepaid Supplies		1,000			
Prepaid Insurance		500	*Owner's Equity*		
		21,500	Owner's Capital account	4,000	
			Retained Earnings	30,030	
Fixed Assets					34,030
Machinery & Equipment	13,000				
Vehicles	6,000				
	19,000				
Less Accumulated					
Depreciation	2,970 *				
	16,030				
Total Assets		$37,530	*Total Liabilities & Owner's Equity*		$37,530

* Since this is the first year of operation for this company, Accumulated Depreciation is the same amount as the Depreciation Expense shown on the Income Statement in Figure 7.7. In future years the Accumulated Depreciation will include prior years' Depreciation Expense.

FIGURE 7.8 Balance Sheet showing how Accumulated Depreciation is subtracted from fixed assets.

GENERAL JOURNAL   Page 3

	date	item	debit	credit
1	12 15	Accumulated Depreciation	9500 —	
2		Fixed Assets		9500 —
3		Retirement of Fixed		
4		Asset		
5				
6				
7				
8				
9				
10				
11				
12				
13				
14				
15				
16				
17				
18				
19				
20				
21				
22				
23				

FIGURE 7.9 After selling a fixed asset, make a General Journal entry as shown here to remove it from the Fixed Asset and Accumulated Depreciation accounts.

Cash

debit (+)	credit (−)
500 (c)	10,000 (a)
	balance = $9,500 credit

Depreciation Expense

debit (+)	credit (−)
9,500 (b)	
	balance = $9,500 debit (depreciation charged over 10-year period)

Fixed Assets

debit (+)	credit (−)
10,000 (a)	500 (c)
	9,500 (d)
	balance = 0

Accumulated Depreciation

debit (−)	credit (+)
9,500 (d)	9,500 (b)
	balance = 0

Selling a Fixed Asset Before It Is Fully Depreciated. As stated above, the book value of an asset is what is left after depreciation is subtracted each year. A $10,000 machine that is depreciated $950 the first year will have a book value of $9,050. After a second year's depreciation it will have a book value of $8,100, and so forth. You may sell or scrap a fixed asset during its useful life either for more or less than its book value at that time. Examples are given below to show you how to record such a transaction (1) when you sell the asset at less than the book value, and (2) when you sell it for more than the book value.

EXAMPLE 1. A $10,000 machine is purchased. Estimated useful life is 10 years. Estimated salvage value is $500. Depreciation method is straight line. At the beginning of the tenth year, the machine is sold for $700. At that time $8,550 has been charged off in depreciation expenses, leaving a book value of $1,450 ($10,000 minus $8,550).

(a) Machine is purchased.
(b) Nine years of accumulated depreciation ($9 \times \$950 = \$8,550$).
(c) Machine is sold for $700.
(d) Loss on abandonment of asset is charged (book value minus sale price is $1450 - \$700 = \$750$).
(e) Machine is written off as an asset.

Cash	
debit (+)	credit (−)
700 (c)	10,000 (a)
	balance = $9,300 credit

Fixed Assets	
debit (+)	credit (−)
10,000 (a)	1,450 (c) + (d)
	8,550 (e)
	balance = 0

Depreciation Expense	
debit (+)	credit (−)
8,550 (b)	
	balance = $8,550 debit

Accumulated Depreciation	
debit (−)	credit (+)
8,550 (e)	8,550 (b)
	balance = 0

Loss on Sale of Assets	
debit (+)	credit (−)
750 (d)	
	balance = $750 debit

107

EXAMPLE 2. A $10,000 machine is purchased. Estimated useful life is 10 years. Estimated salvage value is $500. Depreciation method is straight line. At the beginning of the tenth year, the machine is sold for $1,500. At that time $8,550 has been charged off in depreciation expenses, leaving a book value of $1,450 ($10,000 minus $8,550).

(a) Machine is purchased.
(b) Nine years of accumulated depreciation (9 × $950 = $8,550).
(c) Machine is sold for $1,500. Book value of $1,450 is $50 less than sale price of $1,500, so profit of $50 was made.*
(d) Machine is written off as an asset.

Cash	
debit (+)	credit (−)
1,500 (c)	10,000 (a)
	balance = $8,500 credit

Fixed Assets	
debit (+)	credit (−)
10,000 (a)	1,450 (c)
	8,550 (d)
	balance = 0

Depreciation Expense	
debit (+)	credit (−)
8,550 (b)	
	balance = $8,550 debit

Accumulated Depreciation	
debit (−)	credit (+)
8,550 (d)	8,550 (b)
	balance = 0

Miscellaneous Income	
debit (−)	credit (+)
	50 (c)
	balance = $50 credit

SUMMING UP

Fixed assets other than land must be depreciated over the period of their useful life. Each year's depreciation is charged as an expense and will be included in operating expenses on your income statement. On the balance sheet you will list the original cost of the asset less accumulated depreciation. Land will remain on your balance sheet at its original cost.

* Note: Depreciation expenses of $8,550 were already charged in previous years, so the only way to account for this $50 is to include it as part of miscellaneous income.

108

Accelerated methods of depreciation are applicable only to property having a useful life of three or more years. If this property is not new, then the rate used to depreciate the property may not be more than 150 percent of the straight-line rate.

The only accelerated depreciation method allowed on new real estate (buildings) is the 150 percent declining-balance method. No accelerated methods are allowed on used real estate. For a thorough presentation of capitalization requirements and depreciation methods, see Internal Revenue Service Publication 334, *Tax Guide for Small Businesses,* or consult an accountant.

8
MISCELLANEOUS
ASSETS
AND
LIABILITIES

In this chapter we will present examples of several miscellaneous assets and liabilities that a small business might have reason to record. The assets covered are employee advances (loans receivable), notes receivable, and deposits. Liabilities include loans payable, accrued expenses, and deferred revenues. You may not come across any of these situations in your business, but, in case you do, check out the procedure for handling each one as outlined below.

MISCELLANEOUS ASSETS

Loans Receivable. Loans receivable is money owed to you by parties you have loaned money to. In a small business this generally will be limited to employee advances. To handle this situation, you set up an account in your General Ledger called ''Employee Advances.''

When you pay the advance you list the item in your Cash Disbursements Journal as shown in Figure 8.1. It will then be posted to the credit side of Cash and the debit side of Employee Advances. When the employee pays you back, you list the amount in your Cash Receipts Journal as shown in Figure 8.2. It will be posted to the debit side of Cash and the credit side of Employee Advances.

CASH DISBURSEMENTS JOURNAL

Page 5

	date	payee	check#	total	salaries	supplies	general	gen. acct name
1	3 /	M. Larkin	2134	100 -			100 -	Emp. Adv
2								
3								
4								
5								
6								
7								
8								
9								
10								
11								
12								
13								
14								
15								
16								
17								
18								
19								
20								

FIGURE 8.1 Recording of an employee advance in Cash Disbursements Journal. The $100 will be posted as a debit to Employee Advances and a credit to Cash.

CASH RECEIPTS JOURNAL   Page ___8___

				①		②	③		④		⑤
	date	item		total		accounts rec.	cash sales		general		gen. acct. name
1	3 15	M. Larkin		100 -						100 -	Emp. Adv.
2											
3											
4											
5											
6											
7											
8											
9											
10											
11											
12											
13											
14											
15											
16											
17											
18											
19											
20											
21											
22											
23											
24											

FIGURE 8.2 When your employee pays you back, list the payment in your Cash Receipts Journal. The $100 will be posted as a debit to Cash and a credit to Employee Advances.

At any time the debit balance (debit minus credit) in the Employee Advances account is the outstanding amount owed you by your employees. The debit balance as of December 31, the last day of the accounting period, will be listed on your Balance Sheet as a current asset called ''Loans Receivable.''

Notes Receivable. In order to improve your chances of collection, you may ask a customer who has a large accounts receivable debit with you to sign a personal endorsement, or note, for the amount owed. Upon receipt of a note, an entry should be made in your General Journal as illustrated in Figure 8.3.

You will also set up an account in your General Ledger called ''Notes Receivable.'' When the General Journal entry is posted, it will be debited to Notes Receivable and credited to Accounts Receivable.

113

GENERAL JOURNAL   Page ___1___

	date	description		debit	credit
1	4 1	Notes Receivable		2000 —	
2		Accounts Receivable			2000 —
3		transfer Jenson A.R. to			
4		note			
5					
6					
7					
8					
9					
10					
11					
12					
13					
14					
15					
16					
17					
18					
19					
20					
21					
22					
23					
24					
25					
26					
27					

FIGURE 8.3 General Journal entry for the transfer of Accounts Receivable to Notes Receivable.

When payments are made on the note, they will be listed in the Cash Receipts Journal as illustrated in Figure 8.4. Note that the interest has been listed separately. It will be credited to an account called "Interest Income" and the rest of the payment credited to Notes Receivable. The whole payment will be debited to Cash.

At the end of the year the debit balance in Notes Receivable will be listed on your Balance Sheet as a current asset. The credit balance in Interest Income will be included in your Income Statement as part of revenues.

Deposits. Money you have paid in deposits for rent, telephone, gas and electric, etc., is considered an asset because it is money owed the business. When you

CASH RECEIPTS JOURNAL   Page _9_

	date	item		total	accounts rec.	cash sales	general	gen. acct name
1	5 1	L. Jenson		510 -			500 -	Notes Rec.
2							10 -	Int. Income
3								
4								
5								
6								
7								
8								
9								
10								
11								
12								
13								
14								
15								
16								
17								
18								
19								
20								
21								
22								
23								
24								
25								
26								
27								
28								
29								
30								

FIGURE 8.4 When you receive payments on notes receivable, list in Cash Receipts Journal. Note that the $10 interest payment will be credited to Interest Income.

give out a deposit, list it in your Cash Disbursements Journal as shown in Figure 8.5. You set up an account called ''Deposits'' and post to the debit side of this account, and the credit side of Cash.

When your deposit is returned, list the amount in your Cash Receipts Journal as shown in Figure 8.6. You then post it to the credit side of Deposits and the debit side of Cash.

At the end of the year, the debit balance in the Deposits account is listed as a current asset on your Balance Sheet.

CASH DISBURSEMENTS JOURNAL

date	payee	check#	total	salaries	suppls	general	gen.acct name
6 1	Bell Tel. Co.	2135	50 -			50 -	deposits

FIGURE 8.5 When you pay a deposit, make an entry in the Cash Disbursements Journal. The $50 will be debited to Deposits and credited to Cash.

116

CASH RECEIPTS JOURNAL   Page _14_

	date	item	total	accounts rec.	cash sales	general	gen. acct name
1	12 1	Bell Tel. Co.	50 -			50 -	Deposits
2							
3							
4							
5							
6							
7							
8							
9							
10							
11							
12							
13							
14							
15							
16							
17							
18							
19							
20							
21							
22							
23							
24							
25							
26							

FIGURE 8.6 When your deposit is returned, record it in the Cash Receipts Journal. The $50 will be debited to Cash and credited to Deposits.

MISCELLANEOUS LIABILITIES

Loans Payable. Loans payable is money you owe someone else, and therefore is a liability. When you borrow money, list the amount of the loan in your Cash Receipts Journal as shown in Figure 8.7. You debit Cash and credit an account called "Loans Payable."

When you make a payment on the loan, list it in your Cash Disbursements Journal as shown in Figure 8.8. Note that the interest part of the payment is listed separately. This will be debited to an account called "Interest Expense." You debit the rest of the payment to Loans Payable, and credit the total payment to Cash.

117

CASH RECEIPTS JOURNAL   Page _11_

	date	item	total	accounts rec.	cash sales	general	gen.acct. name
1	8 1	Bank & Trust Co.	3000 -			3000 -	Loans Pay.
2							
3							
4							
5							
6							
7							
8							
9							
10							
11							
12							
13							
14							
15							
16							
17							
18							

FIGURE 8.7 When you receive a loan, enter in the Cash Receipts Journal. The $3,000 will be debited to Cash and credited to Loans Payable.

To avoid the trouble of recording interest and principle separately on each loan payment, you may record all payments as a debit to Loans Payable. Then at the end of the year when you receive a statement from your bank listing the total interest you paid, you credit this amount to Loans Payable and debit it to Interest Expense.

At the end of the year the credit balance in Loans Payable will be listed on your Balance Sheet as a liability. The debit balance in Interest Expense will be listed as an operating expense on your Income Statement.

Accrued Expenses. An accrued expense is an expense you have already incurred but have not yet paid for. An example would be money owed your employees for work performed but not yet paid for, or money owed lawyers and other professionals for services performed. The only time accrued expenses are of concern is when you are preparing financial statements, and then only if you are on an accrual basis of accounting for tax purposes.

Suppose, for example, the year ends on Wednesday and you pay your employees on Friday. When preparing the end of the year financial statements, you have to take into consideration the three days' payroll expense you have accrued.

118

CASH DISBURSEMENTS JOURNAL

Page 10

date	payee	check#	total	salaries	suppls.	general	gen.acct. name
9 1	Bank & Trust Co.	2136	156 –				140 – Loans Pay.
							16 – Int. Ex.

FIGURE 8.8 Illustration of a loan payment. The total $156 will be credited to Cash. The $140 principle will be debited to Loans Payable. The $16 interest payment will be debited to Interest Expense.

119

Here is how to handle it: You make an entry in your General Journal debiting Payroll Expense and crediting an account called "Salaries Payable" (see Figure 8.9). Now your Payroll Expense will accurately reflect the total year's expense on your Income Statement. The credit balance in Salaries Payable will appear on your Balance Sheet under liabilities. At the beginning of the next year you reverse the entry—that is, credit Payroll Expense and debit Salaries Payable (see General Journal entry in Figure 8.10).

FIGURE 8.9 General Journal entry illustrating the recording of an accrued expense.

GENERAL JOURNAL   Page 2

	date	description	debit	credit
1	12 31	Payroll Expense	330	
2		Salaries Payable		330
3		Accrued Payroll		
4		Expense Adjustment		

FIGURE 8.10 At the beginning of the following year, reverse recording of accrued expenses.

GENERAL JOURNAL   Page 2

	date	description	debit	credit
1	12 31	Salaries Payable	330 –	
2		Payroll Expense		330 –
3		Reverse Accrued		
4		Payroll Expense Adj.		

Other accrued expenses are handled in the same manner and entered in accounts called "Sales Taxes Payable," "Legal Fees Payable," etc. However, you must remember to reverse these entries at the beginning of the following year or you will be doubling up on some expenses.

Deferred Revenues. Deferred revenues are payments already received for goods not yet delivered or services not yet performed such as prepaid orders that have not been shipped. Or, if you are a contractor, you might receive an advance before work is actually completed.

Whether or not you are on a cash or accrual basis for tax purposes, you will have to include these revenues as part of taxable income in the year you received them. There are some exceptions to this rule, and you should check with an accountant first if you have received any significant prepayments.

For your own managerial information, you will want your financial statements to reflect the liability to deliver goods or perform services in your next accounting period. To do this, you add up all revenues received for which services have not yet been performed or goods not shipped. You then make an entry in your General Journal as shown in Figure 8.11. This amount will be debited to Sales or Income, and credited to an account called "Deferred Revenues." This will lower the credit balance in your Sales or Income account on your Income Statement. The credit balance in Deferred Revenues will appear as a liability on your Balance Sheet.

FIGURE 8.11 General Journal entry to account for deferred revenues.

	date	description	debit	credit
1	12 31	Sales	1500 –	
2		Deferred Revenues		1500 –
3		Deferred Revenues		
4		Adjustment		
5				
6				
7				
8				
9				
10				
11				
12				
13				
14				
15				

GENERAL JOURNAL   Page 2

At the beginning of the following year, you reverse the entry as shown in the General Journal in Figure 8.12. Sales or Income is now credited with the amount, and Deferred Revenues is debited.

SUMMING UP

Assets such as loans receivable, notes receivable, and deposits may not occur in every small business, but you should know how to handle them if they do. All three will appear on your Balance Sheet as current assets at the end of the year.

FIGURE 8.12 At the beginning of the following year, reverse recording of deferred revenues.

	date	description		debit	credit
		GENERAL JOURNAL	Page 2	①	②
1	1 / 1	Deferred Revenues		1500 –	
2		Sales			1500 –
3		Reverse Deferred			
4		Revenues Adjustment			
5					
6					
7					
8					
9					
10					
11					
12					
13					
14					
15					
16					
17					
18					
19					
20					
21					
22					
23					
24					
25					
26					
27					
28					
29					

Loans payable is a miscellaneous liability that most small businesses will deal with at one time or another. The interest paid on loans is an allowable operating expense.

Accrued expenses and deferred revenues can be accounted for at the end of the year before preparing your financial statements (see Chapter 12). Before recording new entries for the following year, you must be sure to reverse the entries for these accrued expenses and deferred revenues.

9
CASH

In this chapter you will see how to set up a change fund (discussed in Chapter 5) and a petty cash fund. You will also see how to reconcile the balance on your monthly bank statement to your checkbook and General Ledger Cash balance.

CHANGE FUND

If you make change in your daily business transactions with customers, it is a good idea to keep a change fund for each cash register or cash box. This should be a set amount of cash that is left in the register at the end of each day.

Suppose you decide to have a change fund of $50.00. You would then cash a check for $50.00, listing it in your Cash Disbursements Journal as a debit to a Change Fund account in your General Ledger. At the end of each day (or whenever you make deposits), you deposit all but the $50.00 in the bank. When making up financial statements, you add this $50.00 to the amount in the Cash account in your General Ledger to get your total cash.

If you decide to increase your change fund, or get another register, simply repeat the above process: Write and cash a check for the desired amount, enter it in your Cash Disbursements Journal, and debit it to a Change Fund account in your General Ledger.

PETTY CASH FUND

A petty cash fund is useful for most businesses. It allows you to pay cash for miscellaneous small items without writing a check. For example, you might use petty cash for taking a customer to lunch, postage, emergency office supplies, or expenses such as transportation.

When setting up a cash fund, a good procedure is as follows: Get a cash box with a key and put one person in charge of it; write and cash a check for the desired fund amount, say, $100.00; record this check in your Cash Disbursements Journal; and debit it to a Petty Cash Fund account in your General Ledger.

Each time you spend the money in your petty cash box, you should fill out a slip as shown in Figure 9.1 stating which expense account is to be charged. Keep these slips in the cash box and when the cash gets low, total up all the slips and write a check for this amount. You then cash this check, put the cash in the box and when entering the check in your Cash Disbursements Journal, summarize the various expenses that will be charged (see Figure 9.2).

When making up financial statements, the $100 in the petty cash fund is added to the debit balance in the Cash and Change Fund accounts to get your total cash figure. This $100 debit balance in your Petty Cash Fund account in the General Ledger will remain on your books as is until you increase or decrease your petty cash fund.

FIGURE 9.1 How to fill out a petty cash slip.

Amount $2.21   No. 14

RECEIVED OF PETTY CASH
July 7   19 78

For Postage

Charge to Misc. Expense

Approved by
L. Tartacl

Received by
M. Smith

Form No. 700-24 "RENCO QUALITY"

	date	payee	check#	total	accounts payable	salaries	general	gen.acct name
			①			①		gen.acct name
1	2 14	Petty Cash	1035	84 -			34	Owner's Ex
2							26	Postage Ex
3							24	Misc. Ex
4								
5								
6								
7								
8								
9								
10								
11								
12								
13								
14								
15								
16								
17								
18								
19								
20								

FIGURE 9.2 Cash Disbursements entry illustrating itemization of petty cash reimbursement.

THE MONTHLY BANK STATEMENT

When you receive your monthly bank statement, you should proceed as follows: (a) Make sure that every item on the statement has a matching canceled check or deposit slip. Do this while the canceled checks are in the order you received them, as this is the same order in which they will be listed on the statement. If you find any errors, notify your bank immediately. (b) Make sure any additional charges on the statement are correct. (c) List these service charges in your Cash Disbursement Journal as shown in Figure 9.3. You can debit these charges to a Miscellaneous Expense account, or set up a separate account called "Bank Charges Expense."

Checking Off Canceled Checks and Deposits in Your Checkbook. You should sort and arrange the canceled checks in numerical order. Then, for each canceled check, you mark off the check amount on your previous month's outstanding check list and each check written in the current month (in your checkbook). As you do this, you should compare the amounts on the stub and check to be sure they match.

The same procedure is followed for the returned deposit slips. Each one is marked off in your checkbook and the amounts compared to be sure they match.

Statement Reconciliation. You can either use the form provided by your bank (usually on the back of the statement) or a sheet of columnar paper as shown in Figure 9.4. If you have a lot of outstanding checks, there probably will not be enough room to list them all on the form provided by the bank. You then proceed as follows:

1. List the new (end of the month) balance from your bank statement, as shown in Figure 9.4.
2. List the date and amount of all that month's deposits not yet credited by the bank. These will be deposits you recorded in that month's Cash Receipts Journal. If you mailed them to the bank or did not take the deposit to the bank until the following month, they will not yet be recorded by the bank.
3. Add the total deposits in transit to the statement balance.
4. List the check number and amount of all outstanding checks written before the end of the month (these are checks that have not been marked off in your checkbook or last month's outstanding check list because the bank has not returned them yet).
5. Take a total and subtract it from the total obtained in step 3. This figure should match the balance listed in your checkbook.

CASH DISBRUSEMENTS JOURNAL

Page 4

	date	payee	check#	total	salaries	suppls	general	gen. acct. name
1	5 3	City Trust Co.	SC	15 32			15 32	Misc. Ex
2								
3								
4								
5								
6								
7								
8								
9								
10								
11								
12								
13								
14								
15								
16								
17								
18								
19								
20								

FIGURE 9.3 Record of bank service charges in Cash Disbursements Journal.

129

Statement Reconciliation - April, 1977

		①	②	③	④
1	Bank Statement Balance:				2750 39
2					
3	Plus Deposits in Transit:				
4	4/28		345 67		
5	4/29		287 42		
6					633 09
7	Less Outstanding Checks:				3383 48
8					
9	# 2054	20 42			
10	2067	105 27			
11	2068	50 34			
12	2071	182 95			
13	2075	10 52			
14	2078	9 87			
15	2091	35 46			
16	2092	205 42			
17	2096	10 98			
18	2111	18 34			
19	2113	106 72			
20	2118	120 34			
21	2128	87 68			
22	2130	135 43			
23					1089 74
24					
25	Book Balance				2293 74
26					
27					
28					
29					
30					

FIGURE 9.4 Bank Statement Reconciliation. The final balance should match the April checkbook balance and the April balance in the Cash account.

If the balance does not match, you follow a further procedure:

1. Check the figures in your reconciliation.
2. *Add* the deposit in transit total to the statement balance.
3. *Subtract* the outstanding check total.
4. Add the individual figures again. Make sure you have copied the bank statement balance correctly, and that you have subtracted all the service charges from your checkbook balance.
5. Go back to your checkbook and prior month's reconciliation sheet and

make sure you listed all deposits in transit and all outstanding checks on your reconciliation sheet.

6. Double check amounts.

If you still have not found the error, go back in your checkbook to the beginning of the month and recheck each computation (addition for deposits, subtraction for checks).

RECORDING BANK DEPOSITS

Whenever you make a bank deposit, you should always keep a copy of the deposit slip. In addition, you may want to add a deposit column to your Cash Receipts Journal to list deposits as you make them. The number in the deposits column will equal the total of all the individual receipts deposited (see arrows in Figure 9.5).

FIGURE 9.5 Cash Receipts Journal with a column for listing bank deposits.

CASH RECEIPTS JOURNAL   Page 2

	date	item	① total	② deposits	③ accounts rec.	④ general	⑤ gen.acct name
1	2 1	Elcron Corp.	150		150		
2		Smith & Wesson	420		420		
3	2 3	Burnett Co.	180		180		
4		Englewood Corp.	250		250		
5		Asco Products	345 → 1345		345		
6	2 4	Action Co.	155		155		
7		Delwood Sup. Co.	45			45	Supplies Ex
8	2 5	Manwood Co.	265		265		
9		Jingle Corp.	465		465		
10	2 8	Barwood Products	213		213		
11		Benson Corp.	325 → 1468		325		
12							
13							
14							
15							
16							
17							
18							
19							
20							
21							
22							
23							

RECONCILING CASH IN CASH ACCOUNT
WITH CHECKBOOK BALANCE

Periodically you should make sure your checkbook balance matches the debit balance (debits minus credits) in your General Ledger Cash account. This should be done at the end of the month after all posting from the Cash Receipts Journal and Cash Disbursements Journal has been completed. Your checkbook balance after all checks have been subtracted for the last day of the month should equal the debit balance in Cash for that month.

SUMMING UP

A change fund is useful for retail or service businesses that make change daily in customer transactions. When depositing each day's receipts in the bank, leave your change fund intact in the register or cash box.

A petty cash fund is useful in order to provide cash for small miscellaneous expenditures. You should fill out a petty cash slip each time money is spent; replenish the fund whenever it gets low; and summarize the slips and enter appropriate expense charges in your Cash Disbursements Journal when you write a replacement check.

When you receive your monthly statement from the bank, you should check it for accuracy and then reconcile it to your checkbook balance and the balance in your Cash account in the General Ledger. Be sure to subtract service charges from your checkbook balance first, and list them in your Cash Disbursements Journal.

10
PAYROLL

When you hire employees to work in your business, you automatically become subject to various city, state, and federal laws requiring you to withhold income and social security taxes from wages; pay employer's share of social security and unemployment taxes; and provide your employees with worker's compensation and disability insurance.

The first step in becoming an employer is to register with city (if your city has withholding taxes), state, and federal governments. Figure 10.1 shows a federal employer registration form. You will be assigned an identification number which will be used when paying taxes and filing forms. You will also receive an *Employer's Tax Guide* from the Internal Revenue Service and a similar employer's handbook from your state and city governments. You should read these guides carefully to make sure you are complying fully with the applicable withholding, payment, and filing requirements.

HIRING AN EMPLOYEE

When you hire employees, have them fill out a W-4 form (Figure 10.2) on or before their first day of work. You must know their social security number, total

FOR CLEAR COPY ON ALL PARTS TYPEWRITE OR PRINT WITH BALL POINT PEN—PRESS FIRMLY
(See Instructions on Reverse)

FORM SS-4 (3-69)
PART 1   U.S. TREASURY DEPARTMENT—INTERNAL REVENUE SERVICE
APPLICATION FOR EMPLOYER IDENTIFICATION NUMBER

1. NAME (TRUE name as distinguished from TRADE name.)

2. TRADE NAME, IF ANY (Enter name under which business is operated, if different from item 1.)

3. ADDRESS OF PRINCIPAL PLACE OF BUSINESS (No. and Street, City, State, Zip Code)   4. COUNTY OF BUSINESS LOCATION

5. ORGANIZATION Check Type
☐ Individual   ☐ Partnership   ☐ Corporation   ☐ Other (specify e.g. estate, trust, etc.)
☐ Governmental   ☐ Nonprofit Organization   ☐ Other
(See Instr. 5)   (See Instr. 5)
6. Ending Month of Accounting year

7. REASON FOR APPLYING (If "other" specify such as "Corporate structure change," "Acquired by gift or trust," etc.)
☐ Started new business   ☐ Purchased going business   ☐ Other
8. Date you acquired or started business (Mo., day, year)
9. First date you paid or will pay wages (Mo., day, year)

10. NATURE OF BUSINESS (See Instructions)
11. NUMBER OF EMPLOYEES→ IF "NONE" ENTER "0" | Non-agricultural | Agricultural

12. If nature of business is MANUFACTURING, list in order of their importance the principal products manufactured and the estimated percentage of the total value of all products which each represents.   A   %
PLEASE LEAVE BLANK
R   DO   TA

B   %   C   %
FR   FRC

13. Do you operate more than one place of business?   ☐ Yes   ☐ No
If "Yes, attach a list showing for each separate establishment:
a. Name and address.   b. Nature of business   c. Number of employees.

14. To whom do you sell most of your products or services?
☐ Business establishments   ☐ General public   ☐ Other (Specify)

PLEASE LEAVE BLANK →   Geo.   Ind.   Class   Size   Reas. for Appl.   Bus. Bir. Date

---

FORM SS-4 (3-69)
PART 2   DO NOT DETACH ANY PART OF THIS FORM. SEND ALL COPIES TO
INTERNAL REVENUE SERVICE
PLEASE LEAVE BLANK

NAME AND COMPLETE ADDRESS

1. NAME (TRUE name as distinguished from TRADE name.)

2. TRADE NAME, IF ANY (Enter name under which business is operated, if different from item 1.)

3. ADDRESS OF PRINCIPAL PLACE OF BUSINESS (No. and Street)

(City, State, Zip Code)   4. COUNTY OF BUSINESS LOCATION

5. ORGANIZATION Check Type
☐ Individual   ☐ Partnership   ☐ Corporation   ☐ Other (specify e.g. estate, trust, etc.)
☐ Governmental   ☐ Nonprofit Organization   ☐ Other
(See Instr. 5)   (See Instr. 5)
6. Ending Month of Accounting year

7. REASON FOR APPLYING (If "other" specify such as "Corporate structure change," "Acquired by gift or trust," etc.)
☐ Started new business   ☐ Purchased going business   · ☐ Other
8. Date you acquired or started business (Mo., day, year)
9. First date you paid or will pay wages (Mo., day, year)

10. NATURE OF BUSINESS (See Instructions)
11. NUMBER OF EMPLOYEES→ IF "NONE" ENTER "0" | Non-agricultural | Agricultural

12. Have you ever applied for an identification number for this or any other business?   ☐ No   ☐ Yes
If "Yes," enter name and trade name (if any). Also enter the approximate date, city, and state where you → first applied and previous number if known.

DATE   SIGNATURE   TITLE

FIGURE 10.1 Application for employer identification number from the United States Treasury Department.

Form W-4 (Revised December 1975)
Employee's Withholding Allowance Certificate

The explanatory material below will help you determine your correct number of withholding allowances, and will assist you in completing the Form W-4 at the bottom of this page.

Avoid Overwithholding or Underwithholding

By claiming the proper number of withholding allowances you are entitled to, you can fit the amount of tax withheld from your wages to your tax liability. In addition to the allowances for personal exemptions to be claimed in items (a) through (g) below, be sure you claim any additional allowances you are entitled to in item (h) "Special withholding allowance," and item (i) "Allowance(s) for itemized deductions." While these allowances may be claimed on Form W-4 for withholding purposes, they are not to be claimed under "Exemptions" on your tax return Form 1040 or Form 1040A.

You may claim the special withholding allowance if you are single with only one employer, or married with only one employer and your spouse is not employed. If you have unusually large itemized deductions, you may claim the allowance(s) for itemized deductions to avoid having too much income tax withheld from your wages. On the other hand, if you and your spouse are both employed or you have more than one employer, you should take steps to assure that enough has been withheld. If you find that you need more withholding, claim fewer exemptions or ask for additional withholding. If you are currently claiming additional withholding allowances based on itemized deductions, check the table on the back to see that you are claiming the proper number of allowances.

How Many Withholding Allowances May You Claim?

Please use the schedule below to determine the number of allowances you may claim for tax withholding purposes. In determining the number, keep in mind these points: If you are single and hold more than one job, you may not claim the same allowances with more than one employer at the same time; or if you are married and both you and your spouse are employed, you may not claim the same allowances with your employers at the same time. A nonresident alien, other than a resident of Canada, Mexico, or Puerto Rico, may claim only one personal allowance.

Figure Your Total Withholding Allowances Below

(a) Allowance for yourself—enter 1 . . . . _____

(b) Allowance for your spouse—enter 1 . . . . _____

(c) Allowance for your age—if 65 or over—enter 1 . . . . _____

(d) Allowance for your spouse's age—if 65 or over—enter 1 . . . . _____

(e) Allowance for blindness (yourself)—enter 1 . . . . _____

(f) Allowance for blindness (spouse's)—enter 1 . . . . _____

(g) Allowance(s) for dependent(s)—you are entitled to claim an allowance for each dependent you will be able to claim on your Federal income tax return. Do not include yourself or your spouse * . . . . _____

(h) Special withholding allowance—if you are single with only one employer, or married with only one employer and your spouse is not employed—enter 1** . . . . _____

(i) Allowance(s) for itemized deductions—if you do plan to itemize deductions on your income tax return, enter the number from the table on back** . . . . _____

(j) Total—add lines (a) through (i) above. Enter here and on line 1, Form W-4 below . . . . _____

* If you are in doubt as to whom you may claim as a dependent, see the instructions which came with your last Federal income tax return or call your local Internal Revenue Service office.
** This allowance is used solely for purposes of figuring your withholding tax, and cannot be claimed when you file your tax return.

See Table on Back if You Plan to Itemize Your Deductions

Completing Form W-4.—If you find that you are entitled to one or more allowances in addition to those which you are now claiming, increase your number of allowances by completing the form below and filing it with your employer. If the number of allowances you previously claimed decreases, you must file a new Form W-4 within 10 days. (Should you expect to owe more tax than will be withheld, you may use the same form to increase your withholding by claiming fewer or "0" allowances on line 1, or by asking for additional withholding on line 2, or both.)

▼ **Give the bottom part of this form to your employer; keep the upper part for your records and information** ▼

-- Cut along this line --

Form W-4
(Rev. Dec. 1975)
Department of the Treasury
Internal Revenue Service

Employee's Withholding Allowance Certificate
(This certificate is for income tax withholding purposes only; it will remain in effect until you change it.)

Type or print your full name	Your social security number

Home address (Number and street or rural route)	Marital status ☐ Single ☐ Married
City or town, State and ZIP code	(If married but legally separated, or spouse is a nonresident alien, check the single block.)

1 Total number of allowances you are claiming . . . . _____

2 Additional amount, if any, you want deducted from each pay (if your employer agrees) . . . . $ _____

I certify that to the best of my knowledge and belief, the number of withholding allowances claimed on this certificate does not exceed the number to which I am entitled.

Signature ▶ .... Date ▶ ...., 19..........

16—63587-1

FIGURE 10.2 W-4 form which must be filled out by employees on or before their first day of work.

exemptions claimed, and marital status in order to compute their payroll taxes. Employees who are exempt from withholding taxes must fill out Form W-4E as shown in Figure 10.3. Employees should also fill out a city or state withholding exemption certificate or both, if applicable (see Figure 10.4).

PREPARING PAYROLL

A payroll book as illustrated in Figure 10.5 is handy for recording employee hours worked, wages, and deductions. "Fed. O.A.T." stands for Federal Old Age Tax, also known as FOAT, social security taxes, or, most commonly, FICA. In 1976 this tax rate for employees was 5.85 percent of their first $14,100 earned during the year. The employer's tax guide contains a FICA tax table to save you the trouble of computing it.

Federal withholding tax is based on the marital status and number of exemptions an employee claims. Again, tables are provided in the employer's tax guide. Your state and city guides also provide tables for computing state and city withholding taxes.

If you have pension or other insurance programs to which the employee contributes, there is space to list these deductions also in your payroll book. You then add up the deductions and compute the net pay for each employee.

When you pay your employees, you can write a check for the net amount and give the employee a statement itemizing deductions, as illustrated in Figure 10.6. Or you may wish to keep a separate payroll account at your bank, using specially designed payroll checks which come with a stub for itemization of deductions. In this case you would deposit enough money in your payroll checking account to cover your payroll each period. Ask your banker to describe his bank's payroll checking account plans.

PAYING PAYROLL TAXES

You may be required to pay the following payroll taxes:

City, state, and federal withholding, deducted from employees' pay.

Social security taxes (FICA), employees' share plus employer's $(5.85 + 5.85 = 11.7$ percent total).

State and federal unemployment taxes, usually paid by employer.

Federal withholding and social security taxes will be paid in a combined payment monthly or quarterly, depending on the amount due (see your tax

FIGURE 10.3 Employees who are exempt from income taxes should fill out this W-4E form.

FIGURE 10.4 State withholding exemption certificate.

FIGURE 10.5 Page from a payroll book useful for recording employee hours worked, wages, and deductions.

STATEMENT OF EARNINGS

NAME _Sue Smith_

Soc. Sec. Acct. No. _120-30-3486_

Period: From _1/2_ 19_78_ to _1/6_ 19_78_

TOTAL EARNINGS _____ $ _200.00_

DEDUCTIONS		
FEDERAL OLD AGE INSURANCE	11	70
FEDERAL WITHHOLDING TAX	24	10
STATE WITHHOLDING TAX	3	40
HOSPITAL INSURANCE		
BONDS		

TOTAL DEDUCTIONS $ _39.20_

NET AMOUNT PAID $ _160.80_

EMPLOYER _Elco Products_

FIGURE 10.6 Itemized statement showing employees their gross pay, deductions, and net pay.

guide). If you make monthly deposits, you can use a Tax Deposit Form 501 (Figure 10.7), which will be provided you by the Internal Revenue Service. These deposits can be made to any qualified commercial bank or a Federal Reserve Bank (check with your bank to find out if they are a qualified depository).

Every employer must file quarterly returns (Form 941, as illustrated in Figure 10.8) for federal withholding and social security taxes. Any balance of payments due must be paid when filing this form.

FIGURE 10.7 Tax Deposit Form 501 to be used when making monthly deposits of federal withholding and FICA taxes.

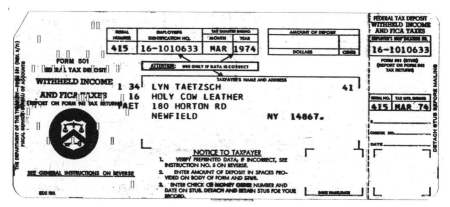

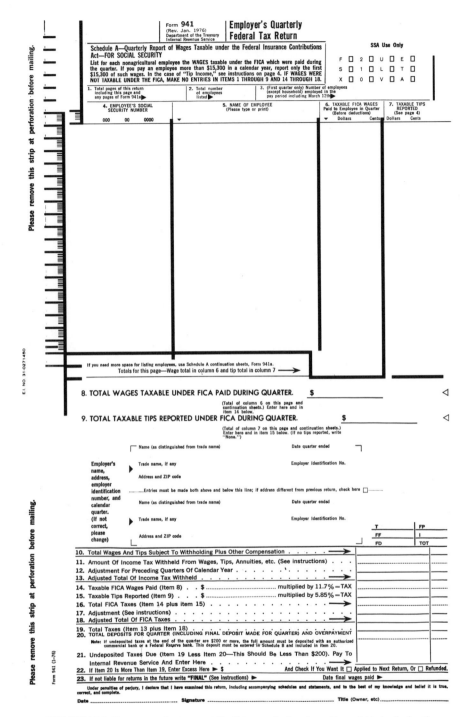

FIGURE 10.8 Every employer must file this quarterly return, Form 941, for federal withholding and social security taxes.

Federal unemployment taxes are payable once a year with the filing of Form 940 (Figure 10.9). You will be given partial credit on this form for contributions to any state unemployment tax fund.

State unemployment taxes may be payable quarterly or yearly, with the filing of an applicable form (see Figure 10.10). Your state tax guide has this information.

City and state withholding taxes may be payable monthly, semimonthly, quarterly, semiannually, or annually. You will file a return like the ones for New York City and New York State that are illustrated in Figure 10.11.

FIGURE 10.9 Form 940 must be filed once a year, accompanied by a check for unemployment taxes owed.

QUARTERLY CONTRIBUTIONS REPORT

READ INSTRUCTIONS ON DUPLICATE BEFORE FILLING IN THIS REPORT

1. (A) Number of covered workers employed during the pay period which includes the 12th day of each month in this quarter......

(B) Number of women on payroll during the pay period which includes the 12th day of the 3rd month ......

2. Total of all wages paid ......
3. Wages paid in excess of $ ......
4. Taxable wages (Item 2 less Item 3) ......
5. Your "Total" Contribution Rate ......
6. Total Payment Due (Item 4 x Item 5) ......

I certify the information in this report is true and correct.

(Signature)   (Title)   (Date)

MAKE CHECK OR MONEY ORDER PAYABLE TO:
NEW JERSEY EMPLOYMENT SECURITY AGENCY
P.O. BOX 1355, TRENTON, N.J. 08625
THIS COPY MUST BE KEPT BY EMPLOYER

FIGURE 10.10 State unemployment tax form.

FIGURE 10.11 Forms for filing and paying New York City and New York State income taxes withheld.

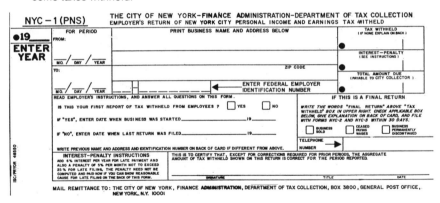

Reminders should be entered on your calendar to compute tax totals and prepare forms so you will make your payments and file forms on time. Failure to do this will result in penalties and interest payments.

W-2 FORMS

At the end of the year, you are required to fill out a W-2 form (Figure 10.12) for every employee, listing the total wages, withholding, FICA, and other tax deductions from his salary (do not include employer's share of FICA). Copies are provided to the employee, plus city, state, and federal tax agencies. The Internal Revenue Service requires a transmittal Form W-3 (Figure 10.13) to be sent with copies of the W-2 forms.

RECORDING PAYROLL EXPENSES

The simplest way to record payroll expenses is to set up an account in your General Ledger called "Payroll Expenses" and charge all salaries and tax payments to it. Whenever you write a payroll check or make a tax payment, you will list it in your Cash Disbursements Journal as shown in Figure 10.14. At the end of the month these amounts will all be debited to Payroll Expense in your General Ledger. This simple method is used if you are on a cash basis of accounting for tax purposes.

If you are on the accrual basis of accounting for tax purposes, you use the above method and make an end-of-the-year adjustment for any salaries or tax ex-

FIGURE 10.12 W-2 form which must be completed for each employee at the end of the year.

142

Form **W-3** Department of the Treasury Internal Revenue Service	**Transmittal of Income and Tax Statements**	**1975**

PAYER'S identifying number	Enter number of documents	Place an "X" in the proper box to identify type of document being transmitted

		Form W-2	Form W-2P	Form 1099R
		21	22	98

30 ☐

Name ▶

Type or print PAYER'S name, address, and ZIP code below (Name must aline with arrow).	All documents are: Place an "X" in the proper box.		All documents are: Place an "X" in the proper box.	
	Original	Corrected	With taxpayer identifying no.	Without taxpayer identifying no.

Magnetic tape or disk pack filers:
See the applicable Revenue Procedures
regarding transmittal of returns on magnetic tape or disk pack.

Under penalties of perjury, I declare that I have examined this return, including accompanying documents and to the best of my knowledge and belief, it is true, correct, and complete. In the case of documents without recipients' identifying numbers, I have complied with the requirements of the law by requesting such numbers from the recipients, but did not receive them.

Signature _____ Title _____ Date _____

DETACH AT THIS LINE

Highlights

Magnetic Tape and Disk Pack Reporting.— We encourage employers and other payers with computer capability to use magnetic tape or disk pack for filing information returns. Many States and localities also accept information returns on magnetic tape, and you may save money by using similar tapes for filing with the Service and with State or local tax departments. Employers find tape or disk reporting allows economy, efficiency, and flexibility. Revenue Procedures on magnetic tape or disk pack reporting of information documents and unified wage reporting using magnetic tape formats are available from most Internal Revenue offices.

Substitute Forms.— Revenue Procedures 75–14 and 75–15 have been issued explaining the format which must be adhered to on all substitute paper forms.

Undeliverable Forms W-2.— Any employee copies of Form W-2 which, after reasonable effort, cannot be delivered to employees should be kept as part of your records for four years.

Instructions—Form W-3

A. Who Must File.— Form W-3, Transmittal of Income and Tax Statements, must be filed by employers and other payers as a transmittal for Form W-2, Wage and Tax Statement, Form W-2P, Statement for Recipients of Annuities, Pensions or Retired Pay, and Form 1099R, Statement for Recipients of Lump-Sum Distributions from Profit-Sharing and Retirement Plans.

B. When to File.— Form W-3 must be filed on or before March 1, 1976.

C. Where to File.

If your legal residence, principal place of business, office, or agency is located in / Use this address

New Jersey, New York City and counties of Nassau, Rockland, Suffolk, and Westchester	Internal Revenue Service Center 1040 Waverly Avenue Holtsville, N.Y. 11799
New York (all other counties), Connecticut, Maine, Massachusetts, New Hampshire, Rhode Island, Vermont	Internal Revenue Service Center 310 Lowell Street Andover, Mass. 01812

District of Columbia, Delaware, Maryland, Pennsylvania	Internal Revenue Service Center 11601 Roosevelt Boulevard Philadelphia, Pa. 19155
Alabama, Florida, Georgia, Mississippi, South Carolina	Internal Revenue Service Center 4800 Buford Highway Chamblee, Georgia 30006
Michigan, Ohio	Internal Revenue Service Center Cincinnati, Ohio 45298
Arkansas, Kansas, Louisiana, New Mexico, Oklahoma, Texas	Internal Revenue Service Center 3651 S. Interregional Hwy. Austin, Texas 78740
Alaska, Arizona, Colorado, Idaho, Minnesota, Montana, Nebraska, Nevada, North Dakota, Oregon, South Dakota, Utah, Washington, Wyoming	Internal Revenue Service Center 1160 West 1200 South St. Ogden, Utah 84201
Illinois, Iowa, Missouri, Wisconsin	Internal Revenue Service Center 2306 E. Bannister Road Kansas City, Mo. 64170
California, Hawaii	Internal Revenue Service Center 5045 East Butler Avenue Fresno, California 93888
Indiana, Kentucky, North Carolina, Tennessee, Virginia, West Virginia	Internal Revenue Service Center 3131 Democrat Road Memphis, Tenn. 38110

If you have no legal residence or principal place of business in any Internal Revenue district, file with the Internal Revenue Service Center, 11601 Roosevelt Boulevard, Philadelphia, Pa. 19155.

D. Payer's Identifying Number.— Your payer's identification number is your Employer Identification Number.

E. Shipping and Mailing.— Employers and other payers filing on the official or substitute paper forms and using more than one type of form should group returns of the same type and forward them in separate groups. For example, a payer of both wages and annuities should file Forms W-2 with one Form W-3 and Forms W-2P with a second Form W-3. Also, file separately forms lacking taxpayer identifying numbers with a Form W-3, and certify that you requested but have not received the recipients' taxpayer identifying numbers.

If you have a large number of forms, you may send them in convenient-sized packages. Show your name and identifying number on each package, number them consecutively, and place Form W-3 in package number one. Show the number of packages at the top of Form W-3. If sent by mail, these forms and packages require first class postage.

General Instructions for Forms W-2, W-2P, and 1099R

A. Who Must File.— The returns to be filed with Form W-3 and the payers responsible for filing them are:

(1) Form W-2, Wage and Tax Statement, is to be filed by employers. (See Circulars A and E for detailed instructions.) However, if you file an Employer's Quarterly Tax Return for Household Employees, Form 942, use it as a transmittal for Form W-2.

(2) Form W-2P, Statement for Recipients of Annuities, Pensions or Retired Pay, and Form 1099R, Statement for Recipients of Lump-Sum Distributions from Profit-Sharing and Retirement Plans, are to be filed by employees' trusts or funds; Federal, State, or local government retirement systems; life insurance companies; and other payers who are obligors responsible for making the reported payments. If an employer makes retirement plan contributions to an employees' trust, which, in turn, is responsible for payments to retirees and their beneficiaries, the trust and not the employer is the obligor responsible for submitting Forms W-2P and 1099R (and Form W-2 for the trust's own employees, if any). These forms should bear the trust's name, address, and employer identification number. (Of course, the trust may employ an agent or fiduciary to prepare and file the forms, while still maintaining its obligor responsibilities.) See paragraph D below. Similarly, a bank serving as fiduciary for an employees' trust or retirement fund and withholding income tax when requested by annuitants, would (if it prepares the Forms W-2P and 1099R) show the obligor trust's or fund's name, address, and employer identification number on the Forms W-2P and 1099R.

B. When to File.— Forms W-2, W-2P, and 1099R must be filed on or before March 1, 1976, except by employers of household workers who must attach

(Continued on page 2)

FIGURE 10.13 Use this transmittal Form W-3 when sending copies of W-2 forms to the Internal Revenue Service.

143

	date	payee	check#	total	purchase	payroll	general	gen.acct name
1	1/14	A. James	1245	342.50		342.50		
2		Ey. Smith	1246	124.70		124.70		
3		L. Harrison	1247	320.65		320.65		
4	1/16	IRS	1248	232.50		232.50		
5								
6								
7								
8								
9								
10								
11								
12								
13								
14								
15								
16								
17								
18								
19								
20								

FIGURE 10.14 List payroll checks and payroll taxes paid in your Cash Disbursements Journal. Debit to Payroll Expense and credit to Cash.

144

penses incurred but not paid by the end of the year. To do this, an account called "Salaries and Taxes Payable" is set up in your General Ledger. If, for example, you owe $250 in salaries and taxes for three days worked in 1976 (for which employees will be paid in 1977), plus $103 in federal withholding and FICA for the last quarter of 1976, plus $98 in unemployment taxes for the whole year of 1976, you would make an entry in your General Journal as shown in Figure 10.15. The total amount of $451.00 ($250 + $103 + $98) would be debited to Payroll Expense and credited to Salaries and Payroll Taxes Payable in your General Ledger.

The $451 would thereby be included as part of 1976's Payroll Expense on your Income Statement and the credit balance of $451 in the Salaries and Payroll Taxes Payable account will be listed as a liability on your Balance Sheet. At the beginning of the following year, you would reverse this entry, as illustrated in Figure 10.16, and continue recording payroll expenses in the simple cash method as described above.

FIGURE 10.15 General Journal entry illustrating an end-of-the-year adjustment for wages and payroll taxes owed.

	date	description		debit	credit
		GENERAL JOURNAL			Page 2
				①	②
1	12 31	Payroll Expense		451	
2		Salaries & Payroll Taxes Payable			451
3		Accrued Salaries (250) with.			
4		Taxes (03) & Unemp. Taxes (98)			
5					
6					
7					
8					
9					
10					
11					
12					
13					
14					
15					
16					
17					
18					
19					
20					

GENERAL JOURNAL   Page 2

	date	description	debit	credit
1	1 / 1	Salaries & Payroll Taxes Payable	451	
2		Payroll Expense		451
3		To reverse Accrued Salaries &		
4		Payroll Tax Expense		
5				
6				
7				
8				
9				
10				
11				
12				
13				
14				
15				
16				
17				
18				
19				
20				

FIGURE 10.16 The entry in Figure 10.15 should be reversed at the beginning of the following year.

STRICT ACCRUAL METHOD OF ACCOUNTING FOR PAYROLL EXPENSES

The strict accrual method is the most complicated; however, at any one time you will know exactly what you owe in payroll taxes.

With this method you will need four accounts in your General Ledger: Salaries Expense, Payroll Tax Expense, Payroll Taxes Payable, and a Payroll Clearing account. When you compute your employees' salaries in your payroll book, you will post the total net salaries paid as a credit in the Payroll Clearing account and a debit in the Salaries Expense account. Total withholding plus employees' share of FICA taxes will be credited to Payroll Taxes Payable and debited to Salaries Expense. Employer's share of FICA will be credited to Payroll Taxes Payable and debited to Payroll Tax Expense.

When you write employees' checks, you will credit Cash and debit the Payroll Clearing account. When you make a tax payment, you will debit Payroll Taxes Payable and credit Cash.

To illustrate this recording process, let us say you have an employee who earns a gross salary of $100. His deductions for federal withholding are $15.00 and for FICA $5.85, or a total deduction of $20.85. Your tax liability (employer's share of FICA) is $5.85. You post from your payroll book as follows:

PAYROLL CLEARING		PAYROLL TAXES PAYABLE	
debit	credit	debit (−)	credit (+)
	79.15		20.85
			5.85

SALARIES EXPENSE		PAYROLL TAX EXPENSE	
debit (+)	credit (−)	debit (+)	credit (−)
79.15		5.85	
20.85			

When you write the employee's check for $79.15, you post from your Cash Disbursements Journal as follows:

CASH		PAYROLL CLEARING	
debit (+)	credit (−)	debit	credit
	79.15	79.15	79.15 *

* Prior entry.

When you make the $26.70 total tax payment (employee's share of $20.85 plus your share of $5.85), you post this amount from your Cash Disbursements Journal as follows:

CASH		PAYROLL TAXES PAYABLE	
debit (+)	credit (−)	debit (−)	credit (+)
	79.15 *	26.70	20.85 *
	26.70		5.85 *

* Prior entries.

At the end of the year, the debit balances in Salaries Expense and Payroll Tax Expense will appear on your Income Statement. The credit balance in Payroll Taxes Payable will be listed as a liability on your Balance Sheet. The Payroll Clearing account will always zero out after posting from the Cash Disbursements Journal. If employees earned monies before the end of the year for which they were not paid that year, you can handle this accrued expense as explained in Chapters 8 and 12.

DISABILITY AND WORKERS' COMPENSATION

As an employer, you will probably be required to take out workers' compensation and disability insurance for your employees. This insurance provides payments for medical care in job-related injuries, plus partial salary benefits while employees are out of work due to these injuries. Employer insurance payments are usually based on the number of employees, level of danger in that particular line of work, etc. Your insurance agent can tell you what the requirements are in your state and how much coverage will cost.

You can record payments for workers' compensation and disability insurance in an Insurance Expense account or in your Payroll Expense account in your General Ledger. It makes more sense to include these payments as part of Payroll Expense, however, since they would not be necessary if you did not have employees.

OWNER'S SALARY

If your business is a corporation, you will include your salary as a regular Payroll expense, taking the necessary tax deductions, etc. If you are a single proprietorship, your withdrawals from the business are not considered part of Payroll expenses, so you set up an account called "Owner's Withdrawal" and post all monies paid to yourself as a debit to this account. At the end of the year, the debit balance in Owner's Withdrawal will be subtracted from Net Earnings to get Retained Earnings (see Chapter 12). If you have a partnership, each partner will have a Withdrawal account in which to list monies paid to him by the business. (See more details on this in Chapter 15 on Partnership Accounting.)

Money taken out of a business by a single proprietor or partners will not have tax deductions taken for income and social security taxes. You, as an individual, will be responsible for paying Estimated Income Taxes and Self-Employment Social Security Taxes. Your Internal Revenue Service agent or Internal Revenue Publication 17, *Your Federal Income Tax for Individuals,* can give you further information on this.

SUMMING UP

As an employer, you have a number of obligations for insurance coverage, tax withholding and payment, and filing various forms. You cannot consider money withheld from employees' salaries as part of your company's capital. Reserves should be kept to cover payroll taxes and payments should be made promptly. The Internal Revenue Service has a strong hand, which includes the right not only to levy penalties for lateness, but to actually close down your business for failure to pay payroll taxes.

11
SALES
AND
USE
TAXES

Many states have sales and use taxes that a seller must collect from consumers and pay periodically. The tax rate will often vary from county to county within the state. Products and services subject to sales and use taxes will vary from state to state. For example, in New Jersey clothing is exempt, whereas in New York State it is taxed.

You should write to your state government and ask for information on sales and use tax laws in your state. The first step is usually to obtain a sellers permit. Figure 11.1 shows a California application for a sellers permit and registration as a retailer. Figure 11.2 shows a Certificate of Authority from the State of New York. These permits or certificates must be prominently displayed in your place of business.

COLLECTING SALES TAXES

If you use sales slips, you must compute the sales tax percentage and list the amount of tax separately from the total purchase amount, as shown in Figure 11.3. When using a cash register, a subtotal of the purchases is taken, then the

**APPLICATION FOR SELLER'S PERMIT AND
REGISTRATION AS A RETAILER
AND
DEPARTMENT OF HUMAN RESOURCES DEVELOPMENT
REGISTRATION AS AN EMPLOYER**

STATE OF CALIFORNIA
BOARD OF EQUALIZATION
DEPARTMENT OF BUSINESS TAXES

1. Office		Date	2. HQ Registration Unit	Date

3. Reinstatement Fee		4. Are You Buying a Business?	5. Date of Purchase	7. Account Number		
Amount	Receipt Number	Yes ☐ All ☐ Part ☐		Tax	Office	Number
$		No ☐ Reorganization ☐	6. Purchase Price $			

8. Owner(s)

9. Firm Name

10. Location of Business:	Street & Number	City or Town	State CA	Zip Code	County

11. Mailing Address (if different from above):	P.O. Box or Street & Number	City or Town	State CA	Zip Code

12. Type or Organization: Husband and Wife Co-ownership ☐ (Describe)
Individual ☐ Partnership ☐ Corporation ☐ Other ☐

13. Corporation Officers:	President	Vice-President	Secretary	Treasurer

14. Name of Former Owner	Business Name of Former Owner	Former Owner's Account Number

15. Type or Nature of Business (If Mixed, Underscore Principal Types and Product)

Check Principal Activity:
Retailing ☐ Manufacturing ☐ Jobbing, or Wholesaling ☐ Repairing ☐ Performing Business, Pro-fessional or Personal Services ☐ Construction Contractor ☐ Type of A.B.C. License

16. Part Time?	Itinerant	Is Business Located Within City Limits?	18. REGISTRATION—DEPT. OF HUMAN RESOURCES DEVELOPMENT

No ☐ Yes ☐ | No ☐ Yes ☐ | No ☐ Yes ☐

Date Started This Address

A. Are you now registered as an Employer under the California Unemployment Insurance Code? No ☐ Yes ☐
B. Do you have more than one establishment? No ☐ Yes ☐
C. Account Number _____
D. Business Name _____
E. Will your payroll exceed $100 in any calendar quarter? No ☐ Yes ☐
F. Quarter ending date Mo.__ Year__ Number of Employees _____
G. Enter first month that worker contributions for disability insurance exceeds $50 OR personal income tax withheld exceeds $100 _____
H. Did you acquire all or only part of the seller's business? All ☐ Part ☐
I. Federal Employer Identification Number _____

17. FOR DISTRICT USE ONLY
Any Delinquencies for Prior Periods? No ☐ Yes ☐
If Yes for What Period? _____
Action Taken to Clear _____
New ☐ Temporary ☐ Issue & Cancel (Attach BT-406) ☐

NO
HRD
COPY
Reinstatement After Revocation ☐
Reinstatement After Revocation & After Close-out ☐
Reinstatement After Revocation & Interdistrict Move (Att. BT-1047) ☐

19.	Basis	Bus. Code	Area Code		Original Starting Date		Owner Code	Account Analysis	FOR HEADQUARTERS USE ONLY							O.S. Audit Office	Local Tax Code	Except. Code	Special Return Processing Code	Ext. Code
			Co.	Jur.	Month	Year			Effective Date			O.S. Location								
									Month	Day	Year	State	City	Zone						
									01											

20. TRANSIT DISTRICT INFORMATION
You are hereby notified that if your location of business is in a transit district which imposes a transactions (sales) tax and use tax, or if you engage in business in such a district (see Section 9 on the reverse of this application and Form BT-741, Your Privileges and Obligations As A Seller, attached), you are required to report the applicable transit district tax on your State, Local and District Sales and Use Tax Return.

22. Furnished to Taxpayer:
Notice of Prepayment Status Form BT-1241 ☐
Form BT-741 ☐
Regulation 1700 ☐
Regulations _____
_____
_____

Returns No ☐ Yes ☐
Periods _____

21. FILING INSTRUCTIONS:
You are further notified that you are required to file sales and use tax returns and pay tax on a calendar _____ basis. Returns are due on or before the last day of the first month following the close of the reporting period.

23. CERTIFICATE: THE ABOVE STATEMENTS ARE HEREBY CERTIFIED TO BE CORRECT TO THE BEST KNOWL-EDGE AND BELIEF OF THE UNDERSIGNED WHO IS DULY AUTHORIZED TO SIGN THIS APPLICATION.

Signature _____ Title _____
Residence Address _____
Date _____
Residence Phone _____
Business Phone _____
Social Security Number _____

DISTRICT OFFICE COPY

STAPLE NUMERIC FILE CARD HERE

FIGURE 11.1 Application for a seller's permit for the State of California.

NEW YORK STATE DEPARTMENT OF TAXATION AND FINANCE - SALES TAX BUREAU

CERTIFICATE OF AUTHORITY

IDENTIFICATION NUMBER

NY 7455731

(Use This Number On All Returns
And Correspondence)

VALIDATED
SALES TAX BUREAU
UNLESS
MAY 2 3 1972
STATE OF NEW YORK
DEPARTMENT OF
TAXATION AND FINANCE

BUSINESS NAME _Holy Cow Leather_

ADDRESS _Apt. 5, 192 Pinckney Rd., RD 7_

Ithaca, N.Y. 14850

is authorized to collect sales and use taxes under Articles 28 and 29 of the New York State Tax Law.
NOT TRANSFERABLE

ST-105 (9-69)   **This Certificate must be prominently displayed in your place of business**

FIGURE 11.2 Certificate of Authority issued by New York State.

		ACCOUNT FORWARDED		
Reg. No.	Clerk			
1	SWEATER		18	35
2	SCARF		5	40
3			23	75
4	SALES TAX		1	04
5				
6			24	79
7				
8				
9				
10				
11				
12				
13				
14				

Your account stated to date. If error is found, return at once.
REDIFORM 56

FIGURE 11.3 Sales slip showing a separate itemization of sales tax.

tax is added. Figure 11.4 shows a "Sales Tax Collection Schedule" provided by the State of New Jersey to help sellers compute sales taxes. If you neglect to collect these taxes as required by law, you are still required to pay them.

RESALE CERTIFICATES

Items that are sold for resale are normally exempt from sales and use taxes. For this reason, wholesalers and manufacturers who sell their products to retailers (who will "resell" them) do not collect sales taxes. Even if you are a retailer, you may occasionally have a commercial customer who presents you with a

153

STATE OF NEW JERSEY
DEPARTMENT OF THE TREASURY
Division of Taxation

SALES TAX COLLECTION SCHEDULE

RATE: 5%		EFFECTIVE MARCH 1, 1970	
Amount of Sale	Tax to be Collected	Amount of Sale	Tax to be Collected
$0.01 to $0.10 ...	None	$6.11 to $6.25 ..	$0.31
0.11 to 0.25 ...	1¢	6.26 to 6.46 ..	.32
0.26 to 0.46 ...	2¢	6.47 to 6.67 ..	.33
0.47 to 0.67 ...	3¢	6.68 to 6.88 ...	.34
0.68 to 0.88 ...	4¢	6.89 to 7.10 ...	.35
0.89 to 1.10 ...	5¢	7.11 to 7.25 ...	.36
1.11 to 1.25 ...	6¢	7.26 to 7.46 ...	.37
1.26 to 1.46 ...	7¢	7.47 to 7.67 ...	.38
1.47 to 1.67 ...	8¢	7.68 to 7.88 ...	.39
1.68 to 1.88 ...	9¢	7.89 to 8.10 ...	.40
1.89 to 2.10 ...	$0.10	8.11 to 8.25 ...	.41
2.11 to 2.25 ...	.11	8.26 to 8.46 ...	.42
2.26 to 2.46 ...	.12	8.47 to 8.67 ...	.43
2.47 to 2.67 ...	.13	8.68 to 8.88 ...	.44
2.68 to 2.88 ...	.14	8.89 to 9.10 ...	.45
2.89 to 3.10 ...	.15	9.11 to 9.25 ...	.46
3.11 to 3.25 ...	.16	9.26 to 9.46 ...	.47
3.26 to 3.46 ...	.17	9.47 to 9.67 ...	.48
3.47 to 3.67 ...	.18	9.68 to 9.88 ...	.49
3.68 to 3.88 ...	.19	9.89 to 10.00 ...	.50
3.89 to 4.10 ...	.20	Over $10	.50*
4.11 to 4.25 ...	.21	Over 20	1.00*
4.26 to 4.46 ...	.22	Over 30	1.50*
4.47 to 4.67 ...	.23	Over 40	2.00*
4.68 to 4.88 ...	.24	Over 50	2.50*
4.89 to 5.10 ...	.25	Over 60	3.00*
5.11 to 5.25 ...	.26	Over 70	3.50*
5.26 to 5.46 ...	.27	Over 80	4.00*
5.47 to 5.67 ...	.28	Over 90	4.50*
5.68 to 5.88 ...	.29	Over 100	5.00*
5.89 to 6.10 ...	.30	Over 200	10.00*

*On amounts above $10.00, the tax shall be $0.05 on each full dollar of the amount of sale, plus the tax on each part of a dollar in excess of a full dollar in accordance with the above formula.

ST-75 (3-70)   IBM Z26018   23721   PRINTED IN U.S.A.

FIGURE 11.4 Most states provide a sales tax collection schedule such as this one to help compute sales taxes.

resale certificate in order to exempt his purchase from taxation. A New York State resale certificate is shown in Figure 11.5.

When you purchase supplies, etc., you may have to present a resale certificate to your supplier in order to exempt the purchase from sales taxes. Your state's regulations should be studied carefully. For example, in one state, inner packaging materials are exempt, but outer packaging cartons are not. If you have any questions, your local sales tax office will supply the answers.

COMPUTING SALES TAXES

If *all* your sales are subject to sales tax and a separate accounting for sales tax collections is not required by law, you can use the following method to compute your sales taxes when due:

ST-120 (1/72)　　　State of New York - Department of Taxation and Finance - Sales Tax Bureau

New York State and Local Sales and Use Tax

To be completed
by purchaser and
given to and re-
tained by vendor.

Read Instructions
on back of this
certificate.

RESALE CERTIFICATE

The vendor must col-
lect the tax on a sale
of taxable property
or services unless
the purchaser gives
him a properly com-
pleted resale certi-
ficate or exemption
certificate.

NAME OF VENDOR

DATE

STREET ADDRESS

Check Applicable Box

☐ Single Purchase Certificate

CITY　　　STATE　　　ZIP CODE

☐ Blanket Certificate

The undersigned hereby certifies that he:

holds a valid Certificate of Authority to collect New York State and local sales and use tax.

is principally engaged in *(indicate nature of business)*..

....

intends that the *(check applicable box or boxes)*

A. ☐ tangible personal property is for resale in its present form or as a component
part of tangible personal property.

B. ☐ tangible personal property is for use in performing taxable services where
such property becomes a component part of the tangible personal property
upon which the services are performed or will be actually transferred to the
purchaser of the service in conjunction with the performance of the service.

C. ☐ service is for resale.

D. ☐ shipping cartons, containers and other packaging material are for resale.
(see special information on shipping cartons, etc. on reverse side.)

understands that this certificate may not be used to purchase items or services which are not for resale and that he will
pay the use tax on tangible personal property or services purchased pursuant to this certificate and subsequently used
or consumed in a taxable manner, and that any erroneous or false use of this certificate will subject him to payment of
tax plus penalties and interest.

SIGNATURE OF OWNER, PARTNER, OFFICER OF CORPORATION, ETC.

NAME OF PURCHASER

TITLE

STREET ADDRESS

Certificate of Authority
Identification Number of Purchaser

CITY　　　STATE　　　ZIP CODE

FIGURE 11.5 New York State resale certificate, which is filed by the purchaser to
exempt purchases from sales taxes.

1. Divide total sales (including taxes collected) by one plus the sales tax rate to
get the sales-only figure.
2. Multiply the sales-only figure by the sales tax rate to get the sales tax. For
example,

Total sales: $8,882.50
Tax rate: 4.5 percent

155

$$\$8,882.50 \div 1.045 = \$8,500 \text{ sales only}$$
$$\$8,500 \times .045 = \$382.50 \text{ sales tax}$$

Check:

$$\$8,500 + \$382.50 = \$8,882.50 \text{ total sales}$$

If only *part* of your sales are subject to sales and use taxes, the following procedure should be followed: Record taxable sales and tax collections separately. If you have a retail business and are using the Daily Summary shown in Chapter 5, add lines 14 and 15 as illustrated in Figure 11.6. If you do not use a Daily Summary, keep a sales tax record as illustrated in Figure 11.7. At the end of the month, total taxable sales and sales taxes; make a sales tax payment if required. At the end of the quarter, compute totals for that period and transfer to tax returns.

FIGURE 11.6 Daily Summary with lines 14 and 15 added to record sales taxes collected.

DAILY SUMMARY

Cash Receipts

1. Cash sales	$325.00
2. Collections on account	100.00
3. Miscellaneous receipts	20.00
4. Total receipts to be accounted for	445.00

Cash on Hand

5. Cash in register:		
Coins	24.00	
Bills	310.00	
Checks	157.00	
Total cash in register		491.00
6. Less change fund		50.00
7. Total cash deposit		441.00
8. Total receipts to be accounted for		445.00
9. Cash short (item 8 greater than item 7)		4.00
10. Cash over (item 8 less than item 7)		—

Total Sales

11. Cash sales	325.00
12. Charge sales (sales slips No. 154–162)	130.00
13. Total sales	$455.00
14. Sales subject to sales tax	$130.00
15. Sales tax collected	$ 5.85

SALES TAX RECORD

date	total sales	taxable sales	collected taxes

FIGURE 11.7 A Sales Tax Record such as this one can be used if you do not use a Daily Summary.

PAYING SALES TAXES

You will probably be required to pay sales taxes quarterly or monthly, and file a return quarterly. For example, in New Jersey you must pay taxes quarterly unless your sales and use tax liability for the first two months of a quarter exceeds $100 per month, in which case you must pay them monthly. A sample of the monthly remittance statement is shown in Figure 11.8. The quarterly return is shown in Figure 11.9.

There are penalties for failing to file returns, or filing late, so you must be sure to comply with lawful deadlines. Generally, even if you do not have any taxable sales in a particular period, you are still required to file a return. You should check the laws in your state carefully.

FIGURE 11.8 Monthly remittance statement for the State of New Jersey.

157

FOR OFFICIAL USE ONLY

75 Z

ST-50 (REV. 12-75)

STATE OF NEW JERSEY
SALES AND USE TAX
QUARTERLY RETURN
MAKE CHECKS OR MONEY ORDERS PAYABLE TO:
NEW JERSEY SALES TAX
P. O. BOX 999
TRENTON, NEW JERSEY 08625

FOR QUARTER ENDING **DEC. 31, 1975** | THIS RETURN DUE **JAN. 20, 1976**

IMPORTANT: PLEASE READ CAREFULLY
1. This return must be filed with the New Jersey Division of Taxation even though no tax is payable or no sales were made.
2. Change in ownership or organization requires a new Certificate of Authority. Do not use previous owner's tax return to file your return. Complete reverse side of this form.

If the business to which this return is addressed will not file future returns, give reason:

If the name and/or address below is incorrect, make the necessary changes and add POSTAL ZIP CODE

If business was sold or ownership was changed give name & address (including zip code) of new owner(s):

NAME
ADDRESS
CITY & STATE
ZIP CODE
DATE BUSINESS WAS TRANSFERRED:

SEE REVERSE SIDE

---

75 T

NEW JERSEY SALES AND USE TAX
QUARTERLY RETURN
READ ALL INSTRUCTIONS BEFORE COMPLETING THIS
RETURN. CHECK YOUR COMPUTATIONS.

1 GROSS RECEIPTS (FOR APR., MAY, JUNE)

2 LESS: DEDUCTIONS (SEE INSTRUCTIONS)

3 BALANCE SUBJECT TO SALES TAX (LINE 1 MINUS LINE 2)

4 A 5% OF LINE 3
B SALES TAX COLLECTED

5 AMOUNT OF SALES TAX DUE (ENTER GREATER OF LINE 4A OR 4B)

6 ADD: AMOUNT OF USE TAX DUE (SEE INSTRUCTIONS)

7 TOTAL TAX DUE (ADD LINES 5 AND 6)

8 If you have paid part of your tax liability for the quarter covered by this return in the form of monthly remittances COMPLETE LINE 8.
LESS: MONTHLY PAYMENTS
FIRST MONTH
SECOND MONTH
TOTAL

9 QUARTERLY AMOUNT DUE (LINE 7 MINUS LINE 8)

10 ADD: PENALTY AND INTEREST (SEE INSTRUCTIONS)

11 ADJUSTED AMOUNT DUE LINE 9 PLUS LINE 10 PAY THIS AMOUNT

I CERTIFY THAT ALL INFORMATION ON THIS RETURN IS CORRECT.

SIGNATURE   TITLE   DATE

FIGURE 11.9 The front and back of a quarterly sales and use tax return for the State of New Jersey.

158

CASH DISBURSEMENTS JOURNAL

date	payee	check#	total	salaries	purchase	general	gen. acct name
3 14	N.Y.S. Sales Tax Bureau	3025	45 32				45 32 Sales Tax Ex
2							
3							
4							
5							
6							
7							
8							
9							
10							
11							
12							
13							
14							
15							
16							
17							
18							
19							
20							

FIGURE 11.10 Page from a Cash Disbursements Journal illustrating the entry of a sales tax payment.

SALES AND USE TAX EXPENSE

DATE 19__	ITEMS	FOLIO	√	DEBITS	DATE 19__	ITEMS	FOLIO	√	CREDITS
3 14	1ˢᵗ Quarter Tax Pmt.	CD-3		45 32					

FIGURE 11.11 The $43.32 sales tax payment from Figure 11.10 is shown here posted as a debit to the Sales and Use Tax Expense General Ledger account.

RECORDING SALES TAX PAYMENTS

If you are on the cash basis of accounting for tax purposes (see Chapter 2), you should record sales tax payments when you pay them—that is, enter the payment as usual in your Cash Disbursements Journal as illustrated in Figure 11.10. This figure will then be posted to an account called "Sales and Use Tax Expense" as illustrated in Figure 11.11. At the end of the year, the debit balance in Sales and Use Tax Expense will be listed as an operating expense on your Income Statement (see Chapter 12).

If you are on the accrual basis of accounting for tax purposes, you should use the above recording method and make an adjustment at the end of the year. If, for example, you owe $68 in sales taxes for the final quarter of the year but have not yet made the actual payment, you make an entry in your General Journal as illustrated in Figure 11.12. When these figures are posted to your General Ledger ac-

FIGURE 11.12 General Journal entry illustrating an end-of-the-year adjustment for sales and use taxes owed.

	date	description	debit	credit
		GENERAL JOURNAL		Page 2
			①	②
1	12 31	Sales & Use Tax Ex.	68 00	
2		Sales & Use Taxes Payable		68 00
3		Adjustment for 4th		
4		quarter Taxes Owed		
5				
6				
7				
8				
9				
10				
11				
12				
13				
14				
15				
16				
17				
18				
19				
20				
21				
22				
23				

counts, your Sales and Use Tax Expense account will be increased (debited) by $68 and your Sales and Use Tax Payable account will show a credit balance of $68. This will appear as a liability on your Balance Sheet.

At the beginning of the following year, after the expense accounts have been cleared (see Chapter 12), this entry is reversed as shown in Figure 11.13. You then continue recording sales taxes when paid, as in the cash method discussed above. (Note that this $68 will be subtracted from the debit balance in the Sales and Use Tax Expense account because it was already expensed the previous year.)

FIGURE 11.13 The General Journal entry from Figure 11.12 must be reversed at the beginning of the following year.

GENERAL JOURNAL   Page 2

	date	description	debit	credit
1	1 / 1	Sales & Use Taxes Payable	68 00	
2		Sales & Use Taxes Expense		68 00
3		To reverse end-of-year		
4		Adjustment		
5				
6				
7				
8				
9				
10				
11				
12				
13				
14				
15				
16				
17				
18				
19				
20				
21				
22				
23				
24				
25				
26				
27				
28				
29				
30				

SUMMING UP

If your state requires the collection of sales and use taxes on various products and services, you must find out how the law affects your business activities and apply for a sellers permit if necessary. Taxes must be collected and a record kept of taxable sales in your Daily Summary or a Sales Tax Record, unless your total sales are taxed at a single rate. Tax payments must be made and returns filed on time in order to avoid fines and penalties.

Sales tax collections must be subtracted from total sales in order to get a net Sales figure for your Income Statement. Sales tax payments must be recorded in an expense account in your General Ledger. If you are on the accrual basis of accounting for tax purposes, you can make an end-of-the-year adjustment to include taxes owed for the final month or quarter.

12
PREPARING
FINANCIAL
STATEMENTS

The first step in preparing financial statements is to prepare a trial balance of your General Ledger accounts. Once the debit and credit totals balance, you will then make any necessary adjustments for accrued expenses, deferred revenues, prepaid expenses, prepaid supplies, depreciation, and inventories. After these adjustments are accounted for, the final debit and credit balances for each account will be used in compiling the Income Statement and the Balance Sheet.

Examples are given in this chapter of financial statements for various types of businesses such as service, retail, and manufacturing. The statements of wholesalers who warehouse inventories will be set up similarly to those of a retail store, since purchasing inventories for resale will be the basis of their profit making. The difference will probably be a larger accounts receivable, larger sales volume, and smaller percentage markup for a wholesaler than a retailer.

Since the largest percentage of small businesses are sole proprietorships, most of the sample financial statements in this chapter are for proprietorships. One set of statements has been included, however, to illustrate a corporation's Income Statement and Balance Sheet. Partnership statements are illustrated in Chapter 15 on Partnership Accounting.

A brief discussion of taxes is included at the end of this chapter, although it is recommended that you get professional help in this area.

MONTHLY TRIAL BALANCE

At the end of every month (after all posting is completed) you should total figures in each account in your General Ledger. In asset and expense accounts, this means taking a debit balance by subtracting the credit column from the debit column total (Figure 12.1). In Liability, Owner's Equity, and Income (Sales or Revenues) accounts, a credit balance is taken by subtracting the debit column total from the credit column total (Figure 12.2). All asset and expense accounts will not always have a debit balance. For example, if you have overdrawn your cash (written checks for more than you have in the bank), you will have a credit balance in Cash. If this happens, the balance is put in the debit column, but with brackets around it.

Every account balance from your General Ledger is listed on a Trial Balance Worksheet as shown in Figure 12.3. The figures in each column are then added and the totals compared. They should match.

If the debit and credit column totals do not match, you have made an error somewhere and must find it: First add the columns again on your trial balance; then double check that you copied the correct amounts from your General Ledger; then check the addition and subtraction in each General Ledger account. If you still have not found the error, you should go back to sources (General Journal, Cash Receipts Journal, Cash Disbursements Journal, Sales Journal, Purchases Journal) to make sure figures were posted accurately, and that the total of the entries from each source zeroes out.

YEARLY TRIAL BALANCE

At the end of the year, a trial balance is taken as above. You then can make any necessary end-of-the-year adjustments to accrue salaries and taxes, adjust sales for deferred revenues, and so forth. These adjustments are discussed in Chapter 8. If you have supplies on hand but have charged all your supply purchases to expense during the year, you may want to count up and value your supplies and capitalize them. This is done by debiting Prepaid Expense and crediting Supplies Expense.

Also at this time you should be sure you have computed this year's Depreciation Expense on assets such as machinery, equipment, and vehicles (see Chapter 7).

CASH

DATE 19___	ITEMS	FOLIO	√	DEBITS		DATE 19___	ITEMS	FOLIO	√	CREDITS
1 31 Jan.	Previous Bal. Jan. Receipts 10,535	CC-1		1,332 5		1 31 Jan.	Disbursements			625 0
2 29 Feb.	" 9,371	CC-1		1,645 0		2 29 Feb.	"			84 32
				1,527 9						1,78 2
3 31 Mar.	" 10,692	CC-2		2,406 3		3 31 Mar.	"			52 73
				7,056						17 7
4 30 Apr.	" 12,496	CC-2		3,71 09		4 30 Apr.	"			20 19
				6,02 3						42 1 9
5 31 May	" * 9,795	CC-2		8,71 32		5 31 May	"			27 6 9 6
				4,034						6,735
				47,726						3,737 1
* This is the balance in this account at May 31.										

FIGURE 12.1 Monthly debit balances are written to the left of the debit folio in this cash account.

ACCOUNTS PAYABLE

DATE 19__		ITEMS	FOLIO	√	DEBITS		DATE 19__		ITEMS		FOLIO	√	CREDITS
									Previous bal.				
1	31	Jan. Payments	CJ-1		405		1	31	Jan. Purchases	5,325	AJ-1		2,705
2	29	Feb. "	CJ-1		21,176		2	29	Feb. "	4,022	AJ-1		3,025
3	31	Mar. "	CJ-2		10,052		3	31	Mar. "	4,376	AJ-2		6,273
4	30	Apr. "	CJ-3		36,813		4	30	Apr. "	12,559	AJ-2		1,406
5	31	May "	CJ-3		41,943		5	31	May "	✳ 14,876	AJ-3		8,735
					29,982								1,073
													3,264
													9,599

✳ This is the balance in this account at May 31.

FIGURE 12.2 In Liability, Owner's Equity, and Income accounts, take a credit balance.

168

XYZ Company

Trial Balance As of 10/31/78

			General Ledger Balance		
			Debit	Credit	
1		Cash	31246		
2		Petty Cash Fund	50		
3		Accounts Receivable	12043		
4		Deposits	100		
5		Fixed Assets	43056		
6		Accumulated Depreciation		12347	
7		Accounts Payable		2310	
8		Notes Payable		30846	
9		Owner's Capital		20000	
10		Retained Earnings		19216	
11		Sales		85432	
12		Misc. Revenues		5076	
13		Purchases Expenses	40144		
14		Salaries Expense	21067		
15		Rent Expense	8700		
16		Utilities Expense	403		
17		Advertising Expense	3725		
18		Supplies Expense	315		
19		Bad Debt Expense	403		
20		Insurance Expense	672		
21		Misc. Expense	803		
22		Owner's Withdrawal	12500		
23			175227	175227	
24					
25					
26					
27					
28					
29					
30					

FIGURE 12.3 Monthly Trial Balance Worksheet.

XYZ Company

Trial Balance As of 12/31/78

	General Ledger Balance		Adjustments		Adjusted Trial Balance	
	DEBIT	CREDIT	DEBIT	CREDIT	DEBIT	CREDIT
1	Cash	6400				
2	Petty Cash	100				
3	Charge Fund	50				
4	Total Cash	6550			6550	
5	Deposits	100			100	
6	Prepaid Expenses		150 ①		150	
7	Accounts Rec.	6420			6420	
8	Notes Rec.	540			540	
9	Fixed Assets	32500			32500	
10	Accum. Dep.		9750		1234 ①		9984
11	Accounts Payable		346				346
12	Notes Payable		11054				11054
13	Salaries Payable				540 ②		540
14	Payroll Taxes Payable				230 ③		230
15	Sales Taxes Payable				150 ④		150
16	Deferred Revenues				300 ⑤		300

170

	Account	Trial Balance		Adjustments		Adjusted Trial Balance	
		Dr.	Cr.	Dr.	Cr.	Dr.	Cr.
17	Owner's Capital		122100				122100
18	Retained Earnings		9935				9935
19	Sales		65425	300			65125
20	Misc. Revenues		540				540
21	Salaries Ex.	43832			540 / 230	43602	
22	Rent Ex.	2900				2900	
23	Interest Ex.	138				138	
24	Promotion Ex.	1300				1300	
25	Bad Debt Ex.	230				230	
26	Sales Tax Ex.	200		150		350	
27	Depreciation Ex.			1234		1234	
28	Supplies Ex.	540			150	390	
29	Owner's Withdrawal	14000				14000	
30		107250	108250	2604	2604	110404	110404
31							
32							
33							
34							
35							
36							
37							

FIGURE 12.4 Year-end Trial Balance Worksheet with adjustments.

Any required adjustments should be posted to the General Journal as illustrated below:

	debit	credit

(1)

| Prepaid Expenses | 150 | |
| Supplies Expense | | 150 |

To record supplies on hand at
12/31/78

(2)

| Salaries Expense | 540 | |
| Salaries Payable | | 540 |

To record salaries from 12/29/78
to 12/31/78

(3)

| Salaries Expense | 230 | |
| Payroll Taxes Payable | | 230 |

To record federal withholding and
FICA expense thru 12/31/78

(4)

| Sales Tax Expense | 150 | |
| Sales Taxes Payable | | 150 |

To record sales
taxes owed on merchandise
sold as of 12/31/78

(5)

| Sales | 300 | |
| Deferred Revenues | | 300 |

To record prepayments by Judy
Zimak for undelivered merchandise

(6)

| Depreciation Expense | 1234 | |
| Accumulated Depreciation | | 1234 |

To record depreciation expense for
the year

All of the above adjustments should be posted to the General Ledger accounts and to the Trial Balance as illustrated in Figure 12.4. The final figures in the Adjusted Trial Balance columns on your Trial Balance Worksheet should

172

match the final debit and credit balances in your General Ledger. All of the above adjusting Journal entries except number 6 (depreciation) should be reversed at the beginning of the following year.

If you are on the cash basis of accounting for tax purposes, the only end-of-the-year adjustment you will be required to make is the one for depreciation.

INCOME STATEMENT AND BALANCE SHEET

You should separate the Income Statement and Balance Sheet figures on your Trial Balance Worksheet as shown in Figure 12.5. The revenues and expense accounts will appear on your Income Statement, as illustrated in Figure 12.6. Operating expenses are deducted from revenues to get the profit (earnings) or loss. Owner's Withdrawals are deducted from this figure to get Retained Earnings (money that will remain in the business as working capital).

The retained earnings for the year will be added to the previous balance in that account (see "Closing Out Income Statement Accounts" below) and the new total will appear on the Balance Sheet (Figure 12.7). Asset accounts such as Cash, Prepaid Expenses, Deposits, Machinery and Equipment, etc., will be totaled on the Balance Sheet. Liabilities such as Accounts Payable, Loans Payable, Sales Taxes Payable, etc., will be listed and totaled. You will then list Owner's Capital and the new total in Retained Earnings. When Owner's Equity is added to the Liabilities total, this figure should match the Assets total.

RETAIL AND WHOLESALE FINANCIAL STATEMENTS

If revenues are generated through the sale of purchased inventories, your General Ledger will include an Inventory and Purchases account (see Chapter 5). To prepare your financial statements, you add an account called "Cost of Goods Sold" and list it on your Trial Balance Worksheet as shown in Figure 12.8. As explained in Chapter 5, Cost of Goods Sold is arrived at by adding beginning inventory to purchases and subtracting ending inventory as follows:

Cost of Goods Sold: beginning inventory
                          + purchases
                          − ending inventory

The inventory figure in your General Ledger will be beginning inventory. This amount should be debited (added) to Cost of Goods Sold and credited (subtracted) to Inventory (see General Journal entry in Figure 12.9). You should then debit the amount in Purchases to Cost of Goods Sold and credit Purchases (Fig-

XYZ
Trial Balance

	General Ledger Balance		Adjustments		Adjusted
	Debit	Credit	Debit	Credit	Debit
1 Cash	6400				
2 Petty Cash	100				
3 Change Fund	50				
4 Total Cash	6550				6550
5 Deposits	100				100
6 Prepaid Expenses			150 (D)		150
7 Accounts Rec.	6420				6420
8 Notes Rec.	540				540
9 Fixed Assets	32500				32500
10 Accum. Dep.		8750		1234 (C)	
11 Accounts Payable		346			
12 Notes Payable		11054			
13 Salaries Payable				540 (A)	
14 Payroll Taxes Payable				230 (B)	
15 Sales Taxes Payable				150 (E)	
16 Deferred Revenues				300 (F)	
17 Owner's Capital		12200			
18 Retained Earnings		9935			
19 Sales		65425	300 (F)		
20 Misc. Revenues		540	540 (G)		
21 Salaries Ex.	42832		230 (B)		43602
22 Rent Ex.	2900				2900
23 Interest Ex.	138				138
24 Promotion Ex.	1300				1300
25 Bad Debt Ex.	230				230
26 Sales Tax Ex.	200		150 (E)		350
27 Depreciation Ex.			1234 (C)		1234
28 Supplies Ex.	540			150 (D)	390
29 Owner's Withdrawal	14000				14000
30	108250	108250	2604	2604	110404

FIGURE 12.5 Figures from the Trial Balance Worksheet in Figure 12.4 separated into Income Statement and Balance Sheet columns.

174

Company
As of 12/31/78

Trial Balance	Income Statement		Balance Sheet				
CREDIT	DEBIT	CREDIT	DEBIT	CREDIT			
			6550				
			100				
			150				
			6420				
			540				
			32500				
9984				9984			
346				346			
11054				11054			
540				540			
230				230			
150				150			
300				300			
12200				12200			
9935				9935 +1521=11,456			
65125		65125					
540		540					
	43602						
	2900						
	138						
	1300						
	230						
	350						
	1234						
	390						
	14000						
110404	64144	65665 -64144	46260	46260			
		1521					

XYZ COMPANY
INCOME STATEMENT 1/1/78 TO 12/31/78

Sales	$65,125	
Miscellaneous Revenues	540	
Total Revenues		$65,665
Operating Expenses		
Salaries	43,602	
Rent	2,900	
Interest	138	
Promotion	1,300	
Bad Debts	230	
Sales Taxes	350	
Depreciation Expense	1,234	
Supplies Expense	390	
Total Operating Expenses		50,144
Net Earnings		15,521
Less Owner's Withdrawal		14,000
Earnings After Owner's Withdrawal		$ 1,521
Retained Earnings, Beginning of Year		9,935
Retained Earnings, End of Year		$11,456

FIGURE 12.6 Income Statement drawn up from the Trial Balance Worksheet in Figures 12.4 and 12.5.

XYZ COMPANY

BALANCE SHEET AS OF 12/31/78

Assets			Liabilities		
Cash	$ 6,550		Accounts Payable		$ 346
Deposits	100		Notes Payable		11,054
Prepaid Expenses	150		Salaries Payable		540
Notes Receivable	540		Payroll Taxes Payable		230
Accounts Receivable	6,420		Sales Taxes Payable		150
			Deferred Revenues		300
			Total Liabilities		12,620
Fixed Assets					
Less Accumulated	32,500		*Owner's Equity*		
Depreciation	9,984		Owner's Capital	12,200	
Total Fixed Assets		22,516	Retained Earnings	11,456	
			Total Owner's Equity		23,656
Total Assets		$36,276	*Owner's Equity + Liabilities*		$36,276

FIGURE 12.7 Balance Sheet drawn up from the Trial Balance Worksheet in Figures 12.4 and 12.5.

177

XYZ
Trial Balance

	General Ledger Balance		Adjustments		Adjusted
	DEBIT	CREDIT	DEBIT	CREDIT	DEBIT
1 CASH	3570				3570
2 INVENTORY	15500		18000 (b)	15500 (a)	18000
3 LOANS REC.					
4 FIXED ASSETS	51600				51600
5 ACCUM. DEP.		10500		1300 (f)	
6 ACCOUNTS PAYABLE		7000			
7 NOTES PAYABLE		10000			
8 SALARIES PAYABLE				200 (e)	
9 SALES TAXES PAYABLE				450 (g)	
10 OWNER'S CAPITAL		23000			
11 RETAINED EARNINGS		10500			
12 SALES		90000			
13 COST OF GOODS SOLD }			15500 (a)	18000 (b)	
14			55000 (c)		52500
15 MISC. REVENUES		600			
16 PURCHASES EX.	55000			55000 (c)	
17 PAYROLL EX.	15000		200 (e)		15200
18 RENT EX.	2400				2400
19 ADVERTISING EX.	1500				1500
20 SALES TAX EX.	630		450 (g)		1080
21 DEPRECIATION EX.			1300 (f)		1300
22 MISC. EX.	400				400
23 OWNER'S WITHDRAWAL	6000				6000
24	151600	151600	90450	90450	153550

FIGURE 12.8 Trial Balance Worksheet for a retail store. Wholesale businesses would be similar, with cost of goods sold computed by adding beginning inventory to purchases and subtracting ending inventory.

RETAIL STORE
As of 12/31/78

	Trial Balance	Income Statement		Balance Sheet				
	CREDIT	DEBIT	CREDIT	DEBIT	CREDIT			
				3570				
				18000				
				51600				
	11800				11800			
	7000				7000			
	10000				10000			
	200				200			
	450				450			
	23000				23000			
	10500				10500	+ 10,220 = 20,720		
	90000		90000					
		52500						
	600		600					
		15200						
		2400						
		1500						
		1080						
		1300						
		400						
		6000						
	153550	80380	90600	73170	73170			
			80380					
			10220					

179

GENERAL JOURNAL   Page 2

	date	description	debit	credit
1	12 31	Cost of Goods Sold	15500	
2		Inventory		15500
3		Add Beginning Inventory to		
4		Cost of Goods Sold		
5				
6				
7				
8				
9				
10				

FIGURE 12.9 General Journal entry to transfer beginning inventory to cost of goods sold.

ure 12.10). Finally, you take the dollar value of your costed physical inventory at year end (see Chapter 5), credit this ending inventory amount to Cost of Goods Sold, and debit it to Inventory (Figure 12.11).

As illustrated in Figure 12.8, these adjustments to the Trial Balance will give you the new Inventory figure and a Cost of Goods Sold figure. When transferring these figures to your Income Statement, you must show how the Cost of Goods Sold was arrived at, as shown in Figure 12.12. The end-of-year Inventory figure will appear as an asset on the Balance Sheet, as shown in Figure 12.13.

FIGURE 12.10 General Journal entry to transfer purchases to cost of goods sold.

GENERAL JOURNAL   Page 2

	date	description	debit	credit
1	12 31	Cost of Goods Sold	55000	
2		Purchases		55000
3		Add Purchases to Cost		
4		of Goods Sold		
5				
6				
7				
8				
9				
10				
11				

	date	description	debit	credit
1	12 31	Inventory	18000	
2		Cost of Goods Sold		18000
3		Subtract Ending Inventory		
4		from Cost of Goods Sold		
5				
6				
7				
8				

FIGURE 12.11 General Journal entry to make the Inventory amount show the year-end inventory, and to subtract this inventory from cost of goods sold.

FIGURE 12.12 Retail store Income Statement prepared from the Trial Balance Worksheet in Figure 12.8.

XYZ RETAIL STORE
INCOME STATEMENT FOR 1/1/78 TO 12/31/78

Sales		$90,000
Cost of Goods Sold		
Beginning Inventory	15,500	
Plus Purchases	55,000	
Less Ending Inventory	(18,000)	
Cost of Goods Sold		52,500
Gross Margin		37,500
Miscellaneous Revenues		600
Gross Profit		38,100
Operating Expenses		
Salaries	15,200	
Rent	2,400	
Advertising	1,500	
Sales Taxes	1,080	
Depreciation Expense	1,300	
Miscellaneous Expense	400	
Total Operating Expenses		21,880
Net Earnings		16,220
Less Owner's Withdrawal		6,000
Earnings after Owner's Withdrawal		$10,220
Retained Earnings, Beginning of Year		10,500
Retained Earnings, End of Year		$20,720

181

XYZ RETAIL STORE
BALANCE SHEET AS OF 12/31/78

Assets			*Liabilities*		
Cash		$ 3,570	Accounts Payable		$ 7,000
Inventory		18,000	Notes Payable		10,000
			Salaries Payable		200
Fixed Assets			Sales Taxes Payable		450
Less Accumulated	51,600		Total Liabilities		17,650
Depreciation	11,800				
Total Fixed Assets		39,800	*Owner's Equity*		
			Owner's Capital	23,000	
			Retained Earnings	20,720	
			Total Owner's Equity		43,720
Total Assets		**$61,370**	**Total Owner's Equity + Liabilities**		**$61,370**

FIGURE 12.13 Retail store Balance Sheet prepared from the Trial Balance Worksheet in Figure 12.8.

MANUFACTURING FINANCIAL STATEMENTS

If revenues are generated through the sale of manufacturing inventories, your General Ledger will include an Inventory and Purchases account. In addition, you will separate manufacturing labor expense from sales and administrative labor expenses. Before preparing your financial statements, you will also assign a percentage of general overhead expenses (rent, utilities, supplies, etc.) to Manufacturing Overhead. Chapter 6 covered these procedures in detail. As explained in Chapter 6, the Cost of Goods Sold in manufacturing is arrived at as follows:

Cost of Goods Sold: beginning inventory
+ purchases
+ manufacturing labor expense
+ manufacturing overhead
– ending inventory

An account called "Cost of Goods Sold" is now added to your General Ledger and Trial Balance Worksheet (see Figure 12.14). The Inventory balance in your General Ledger Balance column on the worksheet is your beginning inventory. You debit (add) this figure to Cost of Goods Sold and credit (subtract) it from Inventory (see General Journal entry in Figure 12.15). Next you debit the amount in Purchases, Manufacturing Labor Expense, and Manufacturing Overhead to Cost of Goods Sold, and credit these amounts to the individual accounts (Figure 12.16). Finally, you take the dollar value of your costed physical inventory at year end (see Chapter 6), credit (subtract) this amount from Cost of Goods Sold, and debit (add) it to Inventory (Figure 12.17).

As illustrated in Figure 12.14, after these adjustments are made, the Adjusted Trial Balance columns on your worksheet will show a new ending Inventory figure and Cost of Goods Sold figure. Purchases, Manufacturing Labor, and Manufacturing Overhead are now cleared (balance = 0) because they are part of Cost of Goods Sold. When transferring figures to your Income Statement, you should show how this Cost of Goods Sold figure was obtained, as illustrated in Figure 12.18. The end-of-year Inventory figure will appear as an asset on your Balance Sheet, as illustrated in Figure 12.19.

		General Ledger Balance		Adjustments		Adjusted
		Debit	Credit	Debit	Credit	Debit
1	Cash	30,000				30,000
2	Accounts Rec.	20,000				20,000
3	Inventory	32,000		30,000 (7)	32,000 (8)	30,000
4	Fixed Assets	90,000				90,000
5	Accum. Dep.		34,000		9500 (2)	
6	Accounts Payable		6,000			
7	Loans Payable		35,000			
8	Salaries Payable				800 (1)	
9	Owner's Capital		45,000			
10	Retained Earnings		30,500			
11	Sales		160,000			
12	Discounts	2500				2500
13	Cost of Goods Sold			32,000 (3)	30,000 (7)	
14				6,000 (4)		
15				5,000 (5)		
16				2760 (6)		94,600
17	Purchases Ex.	60,000			6,000 (4)	
18	MFG. Overhead Ex.	5,000			5,000 (5)	
19	MFG. Labor Ex.	27,000		600 (1)	2760 (6)	
20	Sales & Admin. Labor	22,000		200 (1)		22,200
21	Sales & Admin. Overhead	3,000				3,000
22	Advertising Ex.	2500				2500
23	Depreciation Ex.			9500 (2)		9500
24	Bad Debts Ex.	700				700
25	Misc. Ex.	800				800
26	Owner's Withdrawal	15,000				15,000
27		310,500	310,500	164,900	164,900	320,800

FIGURE 12.14 Trial Balance Worksheet for a manufacturing concern.

MANUFACTURING COMPANY

As Of 12/31/78

	6	7	8	9	10	11	12	13
	TRIAL BALANCE	INCOME STATEMENT		BALANCE SHEET				
	CREDIT	DEBIT	CREDIT	DEBIT	CREDIT			
				30000				
				20000				
				30000				
				90000				
	43500				43500			
	6000				6000			
	35000				35000			
	800				800			
	45000				45000			
	30500				30500 + 9200 = 39,700			
	16000		16000					
		2500						
		9600						
		22200						
		3000						
		2500						
		9500						
		700						
		800						
		15000						
	320800	150800	16000	170000	170000			
			150800					
			9200					

185

	date	Description	debit	credit
1	12 31	Cost of Goods Sold	32000	
2		Inventory		32000
3		Add Beginning Inventory		
4		to Cost of Goods Sold		
5				
6				
7				
8				
9				
10				
11				
12				
13				
14				
15				

FIGURE 12.15 General Journal entry to transfer beginning inventory to cost of goods sold.

	date	description	debit	credit
1	12 31	Cost of Goods Sold	60000	
2		Purchases Expense		60000
3		Add purchases Expense to		
4		Cost of Goods Sold		
5				
6		Cost of Goods Sold	5000	
7		Mfg. Overhead Expense		5000
8		Add Mfg. Overhead to		
9		Cost of Goods Sold		
10				
11		Cost of Goods Sold	27600	
12		Mfg. Labor Expense		27600
13		Add Mfg. Labor Ex. to		
14		Cost of goods sold		
15				
16				
17				
18				
19				
20				

FIGURE 12.16 General Journal entries to transfer purchases, manufacturing overhead, and manufacturing labor to cost of goods sold.

	date	description	debit	credit
			①	②
1	12 31	Inventory	30 000	
2		Cost of Goods Sold		30 000
3		Subtract Ending Inventory		
4		from Cost of Goods Sold		
5				
6				
7				
8				

FIGURE 12.17 General Journal entry to make the Inventory account show the year-end inventory and to subtract this inventory from the cost of goods sold.

XYZ MANUFACTURING COMPANY
INCOME STATEMENT FOR 1/1/78 TO 12/31/78

Gross Sales	$160,000	
less Discounts	(2,500)	
Net Sales		$157,500
Cost of Goods Sold		
Beginning Inventory	32,000	
plus Purchases	60,000	
plus Manufacturing Overhead	5,000	
plus Manufacturing Labor	27,600	
less Ending Inventory	(30,000)	
Cost of Goods Sold		94,600
Gross Profit		62,900
Sales & Administrative Expenses		
Salaries	22,200	
Overhead	3,000	
Advertising	2,500	
Depreciation Expense	9,500	
Bad Debts Expense	700	
Miscellaneous Expense	800	
Total Sales and Administrative Expenses		38,700
Net Earnings		24,200
Less Owner's Withdrawal		15,000
Earnings after Owner's Withdrawal		$ 9,200
Retained Earnings, Beginning of Year		30,500
Retained Earnings, End of Year		$ 39,700

FIGURE 12.18 Manufacturing Income Statement prepared from the Trial Balance Worksheet in Figure 12.14.

187

XYZ MANUFACTURING COMPANY
BALANCE SHEET AS OF 12/31/78

Assets

		Liabilities		
Cash	$ 30,000	Accounts Payable		$ 6,000
Accounts Receivable	20,000	Loans Payable		35,000
Inventory	30,000	Salaries Payable		800
		Total Liabilities		41,800
Fixed Assets				
Less Accumulated	90,000	*Owner's Equity*		
Depreciation	43,500	Owner's Capital	45,000	
Total Fixed Assets	46,500	Retained Earnings	39,700	
		Total Owner's Equity		84,700
Total Assets	$126,500	Owner's Equity + Liabilities		$126,500

FIGURE 12.19 Manufacturing Balance Sheet prepared from the Trial Balance Worksheet in Figure 12.14.

188

Freight Charges. Freight charges for goods delivered to you should be included as part of Purchases expense. You may wish to record them in a separate account in order to be aware of the amount spent on freight. In this case you should make an adjustment at the end of the year transferring freight to Cost of Goods Sold (see Figure 12.20). If you are a service business without inventories, you can include Freight Charges Expense as an operating expense on your Income Statement.

Freight charges on goods you ship out will usually be charged to and paid for by your customers. If, however, you pay these charges, they are part of Sales Expense.

SEPARATING SALES EXPENSES FROM ADMINISTRATIVE EXPENSES

You may wish to keep Sales Expenses separate from General and Administrative Expenses. Figure 12.21 shows an Income Statement where Sales Salaries, Rent Expense for Selling Space, Advertising Expense, Freight Out Expense, Store

FIGURE 12.20 General Journal entry to transfer freight-in charges to cost of goods sold.

	date	description	debit	credit
		GENERAL JOURNAL		Page 2
			①	②
1	12 31	Cost of Goods Sold	125	
2		Freight Expense		125
3		To add Freight to Cost		
4		of goods Sold		
5				
6				
7				
8				
9				
10				
11				
12				
13				
14				
15				
16				
17				
18				
19				
20				

XYZ RETAIL STORE
INCOME STATEMENT FOR 1/1/78 TO 12/31/78

Sales		$100,000
Cost of Goods Sold		
Beginning Inventory	16,000	
plus Purchases	58,000	
less Ending Inventory	(18,000)	
Cost of Goods Sold		56,000
Gross Margin		44,000
Operating Expenses		
Sales Expenses		
Sales Salaries	15,000	
Rent Expense for Selling Space	3,000	
Advertising Expense	2,500	
Freight-Out Expense	100	
Store Supplies Used	500	
Depreciation Expense for Store Fixtures	600	
Total Selling Expense	21,700	
General & Administrative Expense		
Office Salaries	5,000	
Rent Expense, Office	600	
Office Supplies Used	400	
Depreciation Expense, Office Equipment	200	
Misc. Expense	300	
Total General and Administrative Expense	6,500	
Total Operating Expenses		28,200
Net Earnings		15,800
Less Owner's Withdrawal		10,000
Earnings After Owner's Withdrawal		$ 5,800
Retained Earnings, Beginning of Year		11,500
Retained Earnings, End of Year		$ 17,300

FIGURE 12.21 Retail store Income Statement showing Sales Expense separated from General and Administrative Expense.

Supplies Used, and Depreciation Expense for Store Fixtures are listed as Selling Expenses for this retail store. You can either keep separate accounts throughout the year for Sales Salaries and Supplies or make adjustments at the end of the year on your Trial Balance Worksheet.

CLOSING OUT INCOME STATEMENT ACCOUNTS

Income Statement accounts must be closed out (balance = 0) at the end of each accounting period, which will generally be one year. These accounts record the revenues and expenses of a single accounting period and therefore must begin each new period with zero balances. Balance Sheet accounts, on the other hand, continue for the life of the business. Assets are increased and decreased; liabilities are incurred and paid up; owner's equity increases or decreases—all on a continuous basis.

The Income Statement shows *how* the owner's equity was increased (a profit made) or decreased (a loss incurred) in a particular period of time. By making the *opposite* entry for the debit or credit balance in each Revenue, Cost of Goods Sold, Owner's Withdrawal, and Expense account—and a matching (debit for credit, credit for debit) entry in the Owner's Equity Retained Earnings Account—you will end up with zero balances in the Revenue, Cost of Goods Sold, Owner's Withdrawal, and Expense accounts. In addition, you will have added (credited) the Net Earnings minus Owner's Withdrawal to Retained Earnings (note that if Net Earnings were less than Owner's Withdrawal, you will have debited Retained Earnings with the difference).

In your General Journal you should make a clearing entry for each Income Statement account as illustrated in Figure 12.22. These entries were made from

FIGURE 12.22 General Journal entries made to close out Income Statement accounts at the beginning of the new year. These figures were taken from the Trial Balance Worksheet in Figure 12.8.

	date	description	debit	credit
			①	②
1	1 / 1	Sales	90000	
2		Cost of Goods Sold		52500
3		Misc. Revenues	600	
4		Payroll Expense		15200
5		Rent Expense		2400
6		Advertising Expense		1500
7		Sales Tax Expense		1010
8		Depreciation Expense		1300
9		Misc. Expense		400
10		Owner's Withdrawal		6000
11		Retained Earnings		10290
12		To Clear Income	90600	90600
13		Statement Accounts		
14				
15				

Page 4 — GENERAL JOURNAL

191

PAYROLL EXPENSE

DATE 19 7X	ITEMS	FOLIO	✓	DEBITS	DATE 19 7X	ITEMS	FOLIO	✓	CREDITS
1 31	Jan. Payroll	CJ-1		6 00	8 15	Tax Payment Refund	CR-5		1 5
2 29	Feb. "	CJ-2		6 50					
3 31	Mar. "	CJ-2		6 00					
4 30	Apr. "	CJ-3		6 50					
5 31	May "	CJ-4		6 40					
6 30	June "	CJ-5		6 30					
7 31	July "	CJ-5		6 00					
8 31	Aug "	CJ-6		6 50					
9 30	Sept. "	CJ-6		6 40					
10 31	Oct. "	CJ-7		6 20					
11 30	Nov. "	CJ-8		6 50					
12 31	Dec. "	CJ-9		6 30	12 31	To Clear Account	GJ-4		7605
12 31	Accrued Payroll Expense	GJ-2		60					
	# 7605			7620					7620
	** - 0 -								

FIGURE 12.23 Example illustrating how a clearing entry closes out Income
Statement accounts. After the clearing entry of $7,605, the balance equals zero.
Note that the Accrued Payroll Expense of 12/31 is reversed by a credit entry of
$60 on January 1. Then the January Payroll is listed as usual at the end of
January. You will probably start a new page for a new year, but this illustrates
what happens from one year to the next.

the Trial Balance Worksheet in Figure 12.8. When they are posted to the General Ledger accounts, the balances will be zero (see Figure 12.23). Note that the last entry in the General Journal in Figure 12.22 shows the addition of Retained Earnings from the Income Statement to the Retained Earnings account. Now the debit and credit clearing entries will balance. The new credit balance in the Retained Earnings account should appear on your Balance Sheet.

With all Income Statement account balances at zero, and Balance Sheet accounts for Retained Earnings and Inventory showing new end-of-the-year balances, you are ready to start recording next year's transactions—once you reverse any accruals. Adjustments made on your Trial Balance Worksheet for accrued salaries, payroll taxes, sales and use taxes, etc., should be reversed. You credit the expense account and debit the payables account. To reverse deferred revenues adjustments, you credit Sales or Revenues and debit Deferred Revenues. For prepaid expenses, supplies, etc., you debit the expense account and credit the prepaid account. Figure 12.23 illustrates the reversal of 1978's payroll expense accrual. (See Chapter 8 for a complete discussion of these accruals.) Remember that the year-end adjustment to record depreciation expense is not reversed.

MONTHLY FINANCIAL STATEMENTS

Depending on the size and activity of your business, you may wish to prepare financial statements on a monthly rather than on only a yearly basis. The most useful statement to have on a monthly basis is the Income Statement, and you can prepare it monthly without making all the end-of-the-year adjustments discussed above. Inventory can be estimated or taken from perpetual inventory records. It is not necessary to clear General Ledger accounts after making a monthly statement. At the end of the year, you can take a physical inventory and make adjustments to reflect a more precise and accurate picture of the whole year.

INCOME TAXES

Single proprietorships and partnerships are not subject to federal income taxes and normally are not required to pay state income taxes (check with your state income tax department to find out if this is true in your state). The net profit or loss from proprietorships is computed on a Schedule C, Profit or Loss from Business or Profession, and added to other personal income on Form 1040, U.S. Individual Income Tax Return. The information from your Trial Balance Worksheet is used to fill out Schedule C. The IRS Publication 334, *Tax Guide for Small Busi-*

nesses is helpful in filling out Schedule C. This booklet also contains information for filing partnership returns.

Corporations, on the other hand, are subject to federal, and in some cases, state income taxes on earnings. However, as an officer or manager of your corporation, your salary is a deductible expense (see Chapter 10, Payroll). Any profits left after all expenses have been deducted will be subject to corporate income taxes. These will be deducted from Income to get Net Income, as illustrated in the Corporate Income Statement in Figure 12.24. Figure 12.25 shows a Corporate Balance Sheet.

Subchapter S of the federal tax law allows some closely held corporations to be taxed as if they were partnerships. If taxed as a corporation, you will pay personal taxes on your salary, plus corporation taxes on profit, and additional taxes on any dividends you receive. Thus dividends are taxed twice. It is probably best to get assistance from a Certified Public Accountant in order to be sure you are paying the lowest legally allowable amount of taxes on your business's earnings.

FIGURE 12.24 Corporation Income Statement.

XYZ MANUFACTURING CORPORATION
INCOME STATEMENT FOR 1/1/78 TO 12/31/78

Sales		$500,000
Cost of Goods Sold		354,700
Gross Profit		145,300
Operating Expenses		
Selling	41,800	
General & Administrative	83,400	
Total Operating Expenses		125,200
Income from Operations		20,100
Other Income		
Gain on Sale of Machinery		5,700
Earnings before Income Taxes		25,800
Income Taxes		11,100
Net Earnings		$ 14,700
Retained Earnings		
Beginning of year		13,800
End of year		$ 28,500
Net earnings per share (based on		
10,000 shares outstanding)		$1.47

XYZ MANUFACTURING CORPORATION
BALANCE SHEET AS OF 12/31/78

Current Assets

Cash		$ 40,000
Accounts Receivable, less allowance for doubtful accounts of $1,500		32,500
Inventories:		
Raw Materials	20,000	
Work in Process	5,000	
Finished Goods	35,000	
Total Inventories		60,000
Prepaid Expenses		3,900
Deposits		4,000
Advance to Supplier		3,500
Total Current Assets		143,900

Property, Plant & Equipment

Land	10,000	
Building	45,000	
Machinery & Equipment	35,000	
	90,000	
Less Accumulated Depreciation	26,900	
		63,100

Total Assets	$207,000

Current Liabilities

Note Payable to Bank		$ 20,000
Accounts Payable		26,000
Salaries Payable		7,000
Payroll Taxes Payable		4,500
Income Taxes Payable		6,100
Total Current Liabilities		63,600
Long-Term Note Payable		14,900

Stockholder's Equity

Common Stock, par value $10.00 per share, issued and outstanding, 10,000 shares	100,000	
Retained Earnings	28,500	
Total Stockholder's Equity		128,500

Liabilities and Stockholder's Equity	$207,000

FIGURE 12.25 Corporation Balance Sheet.

196

SUMMING UP

The Trial Balance Worksheet is your basic tool for checking the accuracy of General Ledger account balances, making end-of-the-year adjustments, and preparing financial statements. When Retained Earnings for the year have been computed by subtracting Owner's Withdrawal from Net Earnings on the Income Statement, you add (credit) this amount to your Balance Sheet Retained Earnings account and clear (balance = 0) your General Ledger Income Statement accounts. If you suffered a loss, the amount should be subtracted (debited) from Retained Earnings. After reversing accruals (if any), you will be ready to start recording the following year's transactions.

13
MANAGERIAL
ACCOUNTING

Financial statements can do more than simply tell you your net profit for the year. By studying and comparing various parts of these statements, you can get feedback about your business's past performance and make judgments about its potential performance. This chapter will cover several standard measures of liquidity and profitability. You will see how to compare financial statements with those of prior years and other businesses in your field. Noticing trends and changes can help you pinpoint a problem area or recognize outstanding achievement early. The last section of this chapter covers break-even analysis—a good tool for analyzing the effect on profits of different costs, operating conditions, methods of pricing, and other management policies.

SEPARATING CURRENT ASSETS AND LIABILITIES FROM LONG-TERM ASSETS AND LIABILITIES

In order for you to use the management tools in this chapter, your assets and liabilities on your Balance Sheet must be broken down as follows:

Current assets. Cash, receivables, inventories, etc., that will be converted to cash within one year. Prepaid supplies and expenses are also considered current assets.

Long-term investments. Stocks, bonds, and promissory notes that will be held for more than one year.

Fixed assets. Equipment, buildings, and land.

Current liabilities. Debts and other obligations that must be paid within one year.

Long-term liabilities. Debts that are not due and payable until one year from the Balance Sheet date.

Figure 13.1 shows a Balance Sheet with these assets and liabilities listed separately.

MEASURES OF LIQUIDITY

Liquidity means simply the ability to pay your bills. If, for example, all your cash is tied up in assets which cannot be converted to cash easily or you have incurred heavy liabilities, or both, you may have difficulty paying your bills as they become due, and therefore have poor liquidity.

Working Capital. Working capital is the difference between a company's current assets and its current liabilities. Adequate working capital allows a company to carry sufficient inventories, meet current debts, and take advantage of cash discounts. A lack of sufficient working capital has been the downfall of many businesses.

How much working capital you should have, of course, depends on the nature of your business. Cash planning and budgeting (see Chapter 14) will help in this decision making.

ABC Company's working capital (Figure 13.1) is

$$\text{current assets} - \text{current liabilities} = 52{,}450 - 21{,}650 = 30{,}800$$

To get a further perspective on the adequacy of ABC Company's working capital, let us look at the current ratio.

Current Ratio. The current ratio tells you whether your business has enough current assets to meet its current debts, with a margin of safety for possible losses such as inventory shrinkage or uncollectible accounts receivable.

$$\text{current ratio} = \frac{\text{current assets}}{\text{current liabilities}}$$

ABC COMPANY
BALANCE SHEET AS OF 12/31/77

Current Assets				Current Liabilities		
Cash		$20,000		Loans Payable		$ 3,000
Accounts Receivable		12,000		Accounts Payable		17,000
Prepaid Expenses		300		Sales Taxes Payable		250
Deposits		150		Salary & Payroll Taxes Payable		400
Inventory		20,000		Deferred Revenues		1,000
Total Current Assets		52,450		Total Current Liabilities		21,650
Long-Term Investments				Long-Term Liabilities		
Notes Receivable		2,000		Loans Payable		22,000
Fixed Assets				Total Liabilities		43,650
Equipment	25,000					
Vehicles	10,000			Owner's Equity		
Equipment & Vehicles	35,000			Owner's Capital	22,000	
Less Accumulated				Retained Earnings	15,800	
Depreciation	8,000			Total Owner's Equity		37,800
Total Fixed Assets		27,000				
Total Assets		$81,450		Owner's Equity + Liabilities		$81,450

FIGURE 13.1 Income Statement in which assets have been broken down into current assets, long-term investments, and fixed assets. Liabilities have been broken down into current and long-term liabilities.

Using the Balance Sheet items from Figure 13.1, ABC Company's current ratio is

$$\frac{52{,}450}{21{,}650} = 2.42 \qquad \text{(or 2.42:1)}$$

Is this a good current ratio? The rule of thumb is that the current ratio should be at least two to one. If you decide that your current ratio is too low, you may be able to raise it by

1. Increasing your current assets by taking out a loan with a maturity of *more than one year*.
2. Converting noncurrent assets into current assets (for example, selling some of your fixed assets, or taking out a mortgage on them).
3. Plowing back profits (putting more of your profits into retained earnings rather than owner's withdrawal).
4. Investing more capital in your business (your own or other people's).

Acid Test or Quick Ratio. The quick ratio compares "quick assets" of cash, accounts receivable, short-term notes receivable, and marketable securities to current liabilities. Let us look at ABC Company's quick ratio:

> Quick assets: 20,000 cash
>   + 12,000 accounts receivable
>   32,000 quick assets

$$\text{Quick ratio} = \frac{\text{quick assets}}{\text{current liabilities}} = \frac{32{,}000}{21{,}650} = 1.48 \qquad \text{(or 1.48:1)}$$

The rule of thumb for quick ratios is that they should be at least one to one. The ABC Company's quick ratio is about one and one-half to one, which is better.

The above measures of liquidity are guidelines only. For example, if you cannot collect your accounts receivable, or your inventory is made up of obsolete stock, the current and quick ratios will not mean much. Accounts receivable and inventory turnover rates will add further information to your analysis.

Accounts Receivable Turnover. Accounts receivable turnover tells you the number of times per year you collect your average accounts receivable. From this information, you can compute your average collection period, or number of days' sales tied up in accounts receivable. You will need information from your Income Statement (see Figure 13.2) as well as your Balance Sheet for this.

METHOD 1

$$\frac{\text{yearly sales}}{\text{accounts receivable}} = \frac{100{,}000}{12{,}000}$$

$$= 8.3 \text{ accounts receivable turnover}$$

$$\text{average collection period} = \frac{365 \text{ days}}{8.3} = 44 \text{ days}$$

METHOD 2

$$\text{average sales per day} \quad = \frac{\text{sales}}{\text{days in accounting period}}$$

$$= \frac{100,000}{365} = 275 \text{ average sales per day}$$

$$\text{average collection period} = \frac{\text{accounts receivable}}{\text{average sales per day}}$$

$$= \frac{12,000}{274} = 44 \text{ days}$$

ABC COMPANY

INCOME STATEMENT 1/1/77 TO 12/31/77

Sales		$100,000
Cost of Goods Sold		
Beginning Inventory	18,000	
plus Purchases	60,000	
less Ending Inventory	20,000	
Cost of Goods Sold		58,000
Gross Margin		42,000
Operating Expenses		
Payroll Expense	18,000	
Rent	3,600	
Utilities	600	
Advertising	2,400	
Supplies	400	
Sales Taxes	500	
Depreciation Expense	1,300	
Miscellaneous Expense	200	
Operating Expenses		27,000
Net Earnings		15,000
Less Owner's Withdrawal		12,000
Earnings After Owner's Withdrawal		$ 3,000
Retained Earnings, Beginning of Year		12,800
Retained Earnings, End of Year		$ 15,800

FIGURE 13.2 Income Statement used for the analyses in this chapter.

In other words, it takes the ABC Company an average of 44 days to collect an account. Is this good or bad? It depends on what terms ABC Company offers its customers. If its terms are 60 days, having a 44-day average collection period is very good. If its terms are 30 days, it is not so good. The rule of thumb is that the average collection period should not exceed 1⅓ times the credit terms. If the ABC Company offers 30 days to pay, its average collection period should be no more than 40 days ($30 \times 1⅓$).

To get a more accurate accounts receivable turnover rate, you can proceed as follows:

1. Use only credit (not cash) sales for the sales figure.
2. Use an *average* accounts receivable figure.

$$\frac{\text{accounts receivable at beginning of year} + \text{accounts receivable at end of year}}{2}$$

(See Chapter 4, Sales and Accounts Receivable, for a further discussion of the importance of keeping control over accounts receivable.)

Inventory Turnover. Inventory turnover shows how fast your merchandise is moving. It is found by dividing the cost of goods sold by average inventory:

$$\text{ABC Company average inventory} = \frac{\text{beginning inventory} + \text{ending inventory}}{2}$$

$$= \frac{18,000 + 20,000}{2} = 19,000$$

$$\text{inventory turnover} = \frac{\text{cost of goods sold}}{\text{average inventory}}$$

$$= \frac{58,000}{19,000} = 3$$

Thus the ABC Company "turned" its inventories three times during the year, or used up merchandise totaling three times its average inventory investment. Usually, the higher the turnover, the better. It is considered a mark of good merchandising and means that a smaller investment in inventory is required. It means items are moving quickly off the shelves. However, at the other extreme a high inventory turnover can lead to inventory shortages and customer dissatisfaction. You should compare your inventory turnover with that of the other companies similar to yours.

(Note: When using the above tools for measuring liquidity, keep in mind that ratios are not ends in themselves and must be interpreted with care. Since ratios are based on past performance, use them in the light of your best knowledge and judgment about the future. Compare your company's ratios with those of similar businesses. Ask your local or national trade association for published data from members. Also see published ratios and turnover figures such as those put out by Dun and Bradstreet. Be aware, however, that there are different ways of computing and recording some of the items on financial statements, which means the figures for your business may not correspond exactly to those of another.)

MEASURES OF PROFITABILITY

Is your business earning as much profit as it should, considering the amount of money invested in it? A number of ratios have been devised to help you measure your company's success in achieving this financial objective.

Asset Earning Power. The ratio of net profit (earnings) to total assets is the best guide for appraising the overall earning power of your company's assets. For ABC Company,

$$\text{asset earning power} = \frac{\text{net profits}}{\text{total assets}} = \frac{15,000}{81,450} = .184 \quad \text{or 18.4 percent}$$

Return on Owner's Equity. This ratio shows the return you received on your own investment in the business. In computing this ratio, you would use an average owner's equity figure. For ABC Company,

$$\text{average owner's equity} = \frac{\substack{\text{owner's equity beginning of year} \\ + \\ \text{owner's equity end of year}}}{2}$$

$$= \frac{34,800 + 37,800}{2} = 36,300$$

$$\text{return on equity} = \frac{\text{net profit}}{\text{average owner's equity}}$$

$$= \frac{15,000}{36,300} = .41 \quad \text{or 41 percent}$$

It is important to realize that the return on owner's equity for a proprietorship and partnership will usually be higher than for a corporation, because an owner-manager's salary is an allowable expense for a corporation. The owner's equity of a corporation will consist of capital stock and retained earnings. The net profit if ABC Company were incorporated would show the $12,000 owner's with-drawal as part of Payroll Expense and the net profit would be only $3,000. Using this profit figure, the return on equity would be

$$\frac{3,000}{36,300} = .083 \qquad \text{or 8.3 percent}$$

In other words, the owner-manager of the ABC Company in either case is earn-ing $12,000 for his management efforts and 8.3 percent per year return on the $39,300 capital invested in the business. Could he earn more than 8.3 percent by investing this money somewhere else? You may be willing to settle for a low re-turn on equity in order to be doing what you want—running your own business—but you should at least be aware of what your money is earning for you.

Net Profit on Sales. This ratio measures the difference between what your com-pany takes in and what it spends in the process of doing business. The ratio depends mainly on two factors: operating costs and pricing policies. If your net profits on sales go down, for instance, it might be because you have lowered prices in the hope of increasing your total sales volume. Or it might be that your costs have been creeping up while prices remained the same. For the ABC Com-pany,

$$\text{net profit on sales } = \frac{\text{net profit}}{\text{net sales}} = \frac{15,000}{100,000} = .15 \qquad \text{or 15 percent}$$

This means that for every dollar of sales, the company has made a profit of 15 cents.

This ratio is most useful when you compare your figures with those of businesses similar to yours, or when you study the trends in your own business from year to year or month to month. Comparing the net profit on sales for indi-vidual products or product lines is also useful. Such an analysis will help you decide which products or lines should be pushed.

Remember, when comparing your net profit on sales with other companies, again it makes a big difference whether you are a corporation or proprietorship or partnership. Owner's salary is part of net profits in proprietorships and part-nerships, but not in corporations. Most published ratios are for corporations.

COMPARATIVE FINANCIAL STATEMENTS

In order to see changes from month to month or year to year, it is useful to prepare comparative financial statements showing two or more accounting periods side by side, with the amount and percentage of increase or decrease. Figures 13.3 and 13.4 illustrate a comparative Balance Sheet and Income State-

COMPARATIVE BALANCE SHEET FOR 1977 AND 1978

	1977	1978	Increase or Decrease	Percentage Change
Current Assets				
Cash	$20,000	$16,000	$ (4,000)	(20%)
Accounts Receivable	12,000	15,000	3,000	25
Prepaid Expenses	300	400	100	33⅓
Deposits	150	150	0	0
Inventory	20,000	26,000	6,000	30
Total Current Assets	52,450	57,550	5,100	9.7
Long-Term Investments				
Notes Receivable	2,000	1,400	(600)	(30)
Fixed Assets				
Equipment	25,000	34,000	9,000	36
Vehicles	10,000	10,000	0	0
Less Depreciation	8,000	10,000	2,000	25
Total Fixed Assets	27,000	34,000	7,000	26
Total Assets	$81,450	$92,950	$11,500	14
Current Liabilities				
Loans Payable	$ 3,000	$ 600	$ (2,400)	(80)
Accounts Payable	17,000	18,000	1,000	6
Sales Taxes Payable	250	300	50	20
Salaries & Payroll Taxes				
Payable	400	500	100	25
Deferred Revenues	1,000	1,500	500	50
Total Current Liabilities	21,650	20,900	(750)	(3.5)
Long-Term Liabilities				
Loans Payable	22,000	31,150	9,150	41.6
Total Liabilities	43,650	52,050	8,400	19
Owner's Equity				
Owner's Capital	22,000	22,000	0	0
Retained Earnings	15,800	18,900	3,100	20
Total Owner's Capital				
& Retained Earnings	37,800	40,900	3,100	8
Owner's Equity + Liabilities	$81,450	$92,950	$11,500	14

FIGURE 13.3 Comparison of 1977 figures with 1978 Balance Sheet figures for the ABC Company.

ABC COMPANY
COMPARATIVE INCOME STATEMENT FOR 1977 AND 1978

	1977	1978	Increase or Decrease	Percentage Change
Sales	$100,000	$120,000	$20,000	20%
Cost of Goods Sold				
Beginning Inventory	18,000	20,000	2,000	11
plus Purchases	60,000	75,000	15,000	25
less Ending Inventory	20,000	26,000	6,000	30
Cost of Goods Sold	58,000	69,000	11,000	19
Gross Margin	42,000	51,000	9,000	21.4
Operating Expenses				
Payroll	18,000	21,000	3,000	16.7
Rent	3,600	3,600	0	0
Utilities	600	700	100	16.7
Advertising	2,400	3,300	900	37.5
Supplies	400	500	100	25
Sales Taxes	500	700	200	40
Depreciation Expense	1,300	2,000	700	53.8
Miscellaneous Expense	200	300	100	50
Operating Expenses	27,000	32,100	5,100	18.9
Net Earnings	$ 15,000	$ 18,900	$ 3,900	26

FIGURE 13.4 Comparison of 1977 figures with 1978 Income Statement figures for the ABC Company.

ment for the ABC Company. To compute the increase or decrease, you subtract the earlier year from the later year figure. To compute the percentage change, you divide this difference by the earlier year figure.

You should examine changes in financial statements from period to period in order to determine the reason for them and whether they are favorable or unfavorable. It may be favorable, for example, if Sales go up, but not if Gross Profit goes down at the same time. In general, you will find comparative Income Statements more useful than comparative Balance Sheets.

COMMON-SIZE COMPARATIVE STATEMENTS

On a common-size Income Statement, net sales are assigned a 100-percent value and then each item is shown as a percentage of net sales. On a Balance Sheet, total assets are assigned a value of 100 percent and every item is shown as a per-

ABC COMPANY

COMMON-SIZE COMPARATIVE INCOME STATEMENT FOR 1977 AND 1978

	1977	1978	Percent of Sales 1977	Percent of Sales 1978
Sales	$100,000	$120,000	100%	100%
Cost of Goods Sold				
Beginning Inventory	18,000	20,000	18.0	16.7
plus Purchases	60,000	75,000	60.0	62.5
less Ending Inventory	20,000	26,000	20.0	21.7
Cost of Goods Sold	58,000	69,000	58.0	57.5
Gross Margin	42,000	51,000	42.0	42.5
Operating Expenses				
Payroll	18,000	21,000	18.0	17.5
Rent	3,600	3,600	3.6	3.0
Utilities	600	700	0.6	0.6
Advertising	2,400	3,300	2.4	2.8
Supplies	400	500	0.4	0.4
Sales Taxes	500	700	0.5	0.6
Depreciation Expense	1,300	2,000	1.3	1.7
Miscellaneous Expense	200	300	0.2	0.3
Operating Expenses	27,000	32,100	27.0	26.8
Net Earnings	$ 15,000	$ 18,900	15.0	15.8

FIGURE 13.5 Comparison of common-size Income Statement figures for 1977 and 1978 for the ABC Company.

centage of this figure. Comparing Income Statements in common-size form can be a useful analytical tool. Having items broken down by percentages of Sales helps pinpoint their relative change.

For example, in Figure 13.5 you will see that cost of goods sold changed from 58 percent of sales in 1977 to 57.5 percent in 1978; advertising changed from 2.4 percent of sales in 1977 to 2.8 percent in 1978; and so on.

BREAK-EVEN ANALYSIS

The "break-even point" is the point of sales volume at which sales revenues just cover costs, with no profit and no loss. Break-even analysis can show at what approximate level of sales a new product will pay for itself and begin to bring in a profit. It is also helpful in analyzing the profitability of products already being sold. Suppose you have a product that has passed its peak in popularity. It is still fairly profitable, but the demand for it is slacking off. Break-even analysis can show you about how far sales can drop before the item will stop making any profit at all, and below what level it will no longer cover even its fixed costs.

Break-even analysis helps to answer questions such as

1. How many units of the new product will have to be sold, given estimates of its cost and selling price, if we are to break even?
2. The change we are planning will mean a 10-percent increase in fixed costs. What effect will this have on profits?
3. What will be the effect of a 5-percent reduction in selling price (or a 15-percent decline in the number of units sold)?
4. How much more will we have to sell to make up for a 15-cent hourly increase in wages?
5. If we buy the new machine we are considering (or truck, or building improvement), how long will it be before the investment pays for itself and begins to return a profit?

THREE TYPES OF COSTS

Costs can be classified as fixed, variable, or semivariable. Fixed costs do not vary with the level of business activity. Examples of fixed costs are sales and administrative (not plant) salaries, property insurance, property taxes, depreciation expense, management salaries, and so on. No matter how much business you do, they stay the same. Variable costs vary directly with the volume of business activity. They double when production is doubled, or drop to zero if there is no production. Plant (manufacturing) labor and materials are examples of variable costs for a manufacturer. Cost of goods sold is a variable cost for a retailer or wholesaler; the more he sells, the more inventory he uses up, thereby directly increasing his cost of goods sold. For example, if cost of goods sold is $60.00 for $100.00 worth of sales, it will probably take $120.00 cost of goods sold for $200 worth of sales:

$$2 \times 100 = 200 \qquad 2 \times 60 = 120$$

Semivariable costs change with the level of business activity, but not in direct proportion. Office equipment might be an example, or salespeople's salaries. Up to a point these costs are about the same regardless of sales. Beyond that point, they go up. A salesperson, for example, might be able to handle an increase in sales up to a certain point, but beyond that there may be too many customers for him to handle efficiently alone. A full- or part-time assistant may have to be hired.

210

You will have to break down semivariable costs into their fixed and variable components in order to use the break-even formula.

FINDING THE BREAK-EVEN POINT

Once you have identified and classified all costs as fixed or variable, you can find the break-even point by using the following formula:

$$\text{break-even volume} = \frac{\text{total fixed costs}}{\text{selling price} - \text{variable costs per unit}}$$

Suppose the RJK Manufacturing Company has figured the costs on one of its products as follows:

Total fixed costs: $40,000
Variable costs: $20 per unit

The selling price is $40 per unit.

$$\text{break-even volume} = \frac{40,000}{40-20} = 2,000 \text{ units}$$

This means that 2,000 units will have to be sold just to break even:

Costs on 2,000 units: 40,000 fixed costs
+ 40,000 variable costs (2,000 × 20)
80,000 total costs
Sales revenue: 80,000 (2,000 units × 40 sales price per unit)
− 80,000 total costs
0 profit

The more units the RJK Manufacturing Company sells beyond 2,000, the greater percentage of profit they will make on the items (provided fixed costs remain the same). For example, (a) If 3,000 units are sold,

Sales revenue: 120,000 (3,000 × 40)
Total costs: 100,000 (40,000 + 3,000 × 20)
Profit: 20,000

(b) If 6,000 units are sold,

Sales revenue: 240,000 (6,000 × 40)
Total costs: 160,000 (40,000 + 6,000 × 20)
Profit: 80,000

211

Note that sales doubled from 3,000 to 6,000 units, whereas profit quadrupled from $20,000 to $80,000. This is because the only cost for the 3,000 additional units was the variable cost of $60,000 (3,000 × $20) and the additional revenue was $120,000 (3,000 × $40).

At some point as sales increase, fixed costs will probably change. For example, you can only display so much merchandise in a certain amount of square feet of selling space. Or when a machine is being utilized 24 hours a day, you cannot increase production without buying another machine.

Another way to use break-even analysis is when you want to know what your minimum sales will have to be in order to break even. Suppose, for example, you are in the mail-order business. You want to place an ad for gidgets. The ad will cost $500. You want to know how many orders (sales) you will need for this ad in order to break even (cover all your costs). You pay $2.00 for each gidget, plus 25 cents each for mailing and handling. Your sales price is $5.00 each. How many orders must you get to break even?

Fixed costs:	500 ad
Variable costs per unit:	2.00 cost of gidget
	.25 mailing and handling
	2.25 total variable costs

$$\text{break-even volume} = \frac{\text{total fixed costs}}{\text{selling price} - \text{variable costs per unit}}$$

$$= \frac{500}{5.00 - 2.25} = 182 \text{ units}$$

In other words, 182 orders generated by this ad will cover the cost of the ad plus all costs of supplying the 182 gidgets.

By being aware of fixed and variable costs and their relationship to increases and decreases in sales or production volume, you will be able to plan better for future expansion of your business.

SUMMING UP

Managerial accounting consists of taking the financial information you have compiled for your business and analyzing it. Measures of liquidity, measures of profitability, comparative financial statements, and break-even analysis are all tools you can use to help you make decisions about the future direction your business should take.

14

CASH
BUDGETING
AND
FINANCIAL
PLANNING

Preparing a cash budget is simply listing how much cash you expect to come in, to go out, and to have left over (or under). By seeing ahead of time that you will have extra cash, you can plan for short-term investments. If you see that you will be short in the future, you can start to plan for short-term loans. If you see that you will be short of cash over a long period, you may need a long-term loan or further capital investment; another solution to a cash shortage is to cut back on expansions such as the purchase of a new asset or opening of a new store.

Although the cash budget will show you where your money is going and how much is needed each month (year), financial planning includes the preparation of a projected income statement and balance sheet. The income statement is especially important. Listing expected sales and expenses helps you decide how much cash you will need. It also gives you something by which to measure actual performance. A projected balance sheet puts in black and white exactly where you expect your company to stand in terms of assets and liabilities in one year.

Taken together, the cash budget and projected financial statements give you an overall picture of your company's future, in terms of cash flow, investment potential, borrowing needs, asset acquisitions, marketing goals, and operating expense limits. By applying the managerial accounting tools discussed in Chapter 13 to your financial planning, in addition to your own experience and judgment, you will be in a better position to foresee problems and take advantage of opportunities in your company's future.

CASH BUDGET

You should set up a cash budget form as illustrated in Figure 14.1. The example is for a three-month cash budget, but you can set one up for the entire year if you wish. You first list all the items that bring in cash, then the expected outlays of cash, and, finally, the balance. If your cash balance is negative, or too low to allow a safe margin, you should consider a short-term loan. If you have extra cash, you can consider a short-term investment.

The balance at the end of one month becomes the beginning balance of the following month. Note that there is a column in which to list your *actual* cash receipts and payments as they occur. These actual figures can be used to make any necessary modifications in the following months' budgets. If you find your budget out of line with what actually is happening, it is time to find out what is going wrong. Are sales much lower or greater than you expected? Are you having difficulty collecting accounts receivable? Have any of your expenses risen drastically?

As mentioned in Chapter 13, having enough working capital to pay your bills is crucial to the success of your business. If you are constantly scraping the barrel for cash to meet a payroll or pay a creditor—getting by by the skin of your teeth—you are putting your whole business in jeopardy. A banker will think more favorably of your loan request if you make it three months *before* a crisis arises rather than the day *after* it happens.

Although we generally expect most problems to arise in the area of not having *enough* cash, sometimes the opposite happens. Leaving large sums of unnecessary capital in your business checking account is a waste. If the measures of liquidity in Chapter 13 tell you that you have much more working capital than necessary, especially in cash form, you should consider putting this capital to work in some short-term investments. By being *too* conservative, you may miss an opportunity to have your investment work to capacity for you.

PROJECTED INCOME STATEMENT

Figure 14.2 illustrates a projected Income Statement for a service business. Figure 14.3 shows one for a retail operation (the same format applies to wholesale businesses). The easiest way to prepare projected Income Statements is to base your plans on what happened in the past. If sales have increased 10 percent a year

214

CASH BUDGET

For three months ending March 31, 19 _____

	JANUARY		FEBRUARY		MARCH	
	Budget	Actual	Budget	Actual	Budget	Actual
Beg. Balance						
Cash Receipts:						
Cash Sales						
A.R. Collect.						
Other Income						
Total Cash Rec.						
Cash Payments:						
Purchases						
Payroll						
Rent						
Utilities						
Advertising						
Loan Paymts.						
Sales Taxes						
Asset Purch.						
Supplies						
Misc.						
Total Cash Pmts:						
Ending. Bal.						

FIGURE 14.1 Three-month Cash Budget Form. You may wish to prepare one for six or twelve months at a time.

215

DEF SERVICE COMPANY
PROJECTED INCOME STATEMENT
FOR 1/1/78 TO 12/31/78

Revenues		$40,000
Operating Expenses		
Salaries	12,000	
Supplies	2,200	
Rent	3,000	
Utilities	600	
Advertising	2,500	
Depreciation Expense	900	
Interest Expense	300	
Insurance Expense	400	
Miscellaneous Expense	800	
Total Operating Expenses		22,700
Net Earnings		$17,300

FIGURE 14.2 Projected Income Statement for a service business.

over the last four years, you can use this information to prepare your projected sales figure. Then you can use the percentages of sales from your common-size Income Statement (see Chapter 13) to compute cost of goods sold, operating expenses, etc. For example, if 1977 sales are $100,000 and you expect a 10-percent increase in 1978,

10 percent of $100,000 = $10,000
$100,000 + $10,000 = $110,000 sales projected for 1978

If advertising expenses have always been four percent of sales in the past,

four percent of $110,000 = .04 × $110,000
= $4,400 projected advertising expense for 1978

The past cannot always be used to predict the future, however. Sales increases do not just "happen" by themselves. During an economic downturn, sales may decline. With the introduction of a better marketing plan, sales may shoot ahead of past performance. So you need to use your judgment about the economy, competition, increases in sales force, new product lines, etc., when choosing a sales figure for your projected Income Statement.

After that, you can use the percentages in your common-size Income Statement as a guideline for the rest of the figures. Here, too, if you know that merchandise prices are going up faster than the sales prices, you may have to

216

IJK RETAIL STORE
PROJECTED INCOME STATEMENT
FOR 1/1/78 TO 12/31/78

Gross Sales	$83,200	$
Less Sales Taxes	(3,200)	
Net Sales		80,000
Cost of Goods Sold		
Beginning Inventory	15,000	
plus Purchases	51,000	
less Ending Inventory	(16,000)	
Cost of Goods Sold		50,000
Gross Profit Margin		30,000
Operating Expenses		
Salaries	7,000	
Rent	3,600	
Utilities	400	
Advertising	2,400	
Depreciation Expense	600	
Interest Expense	100	
Supplies Expense	200	
Insurance Expense	400	
Total Operating Expenses		14,700
Net Earnings		$15,300

FIGURE 14.3 Projected Income Statement for a retail store.

allot a greater percentage for cost of goods sold. In another instance you may have purchased a machine that will eliminate some of your labor costs, making this figure lower, but depreciation expenses higher. So use your common-size Income Statement as a guide, but add input from your own knowledge and management plans for the future.

PROJECTED BALANCE SHEET

Figure 14.4 shows a projected Balance Sheet for the DEF Service Company. Figure 14.5 shows one for the IJK Retail Store. To prepare a projected Balance Sheet, begin with the last actual Balance Sheet you prepared. Some items may remain the same, while others will change.

DEF SERVICE COMPANY
PROJECTED BALANCE SHEET AS OF 12/31/78

Current Assets			*Current Liabilities*		
Cash		$ 6,000	Salaries Payable		$ 150
Deposits		100	Notes Payable		250
Prepaid Supplies		200	Total Current Liabilities		400
Total Current Assets		6,300			
			Long-Term Liabilities		
			Loans Payable		20,000
Fixed Assets					
Equipment	40,000		*Total Liabilities*		20,400
Vehicle	12,000				
Equipment & Vehicles	52,000		*Owner's Equity*		
Less Accumulated			Owner's Capital	15,000	
Depreciation	10,000		Retained Earnings	12,900	
Total Fixed Assets		42,000	Total Owner's Equity		27,900
Total Assets		$48,300	*Owner's Equity + Liabilities*		$48,300

FIGURE 14.4 Projected Balance Sheet for a service business.

IJK RETAIL STORE

PROJECTED BALANCE SHEET AS OF 12/31/78

Current Assets		*Current Liabilities*	
Cash	$10,000	Accounts Payable	$ 8,000
Inventory	16,000	Notes Payable	600
Prepaid Expenses	300	Salaries Payable	200
Total Current Assets	26,300	Sales Taxes Payable	500
		Total Current Liabilities	9,300
Fixed Assets			
Store Equipment	48,000	*Long-Term Liabilities*	
Vehicle	8,000	Loans Payable	26,000
Equipment & Vehicles	56,000		
Less Accumulated		*Total Liabilities*	35,300
Depreciation	12,000		
Total Fixed Assets	44,000	*Owner's Equity*	
		Owner's Capital 20,000	
		Retained Earnings 15,000	
		Total Owner's Equity	35,000
Total Assets	$70,300	*Owner's Equity + Liabilities*	$70,300

FIGURE 14.5 Projected Balance Sheet for a retail store.

219

Fixed assets will remain the same except for accumulated depreciation, which will be higher (add the depreciation expense from your projected Income Statement). If you plan to buy additional fixed assets, total fixed assets will increase by the purchase price of the asset. For example, if you purchase a $10,000 machine and fixed assets were $40,000 at the end of the year, they will be $50,000 on the projected Balance Sheet for the following year (be sure to add the extra depreciation expense for this $10,000 machine to accumulated depreciation).

Accounts receivable will probably increase proportionately as credit sales increase, unless there is some other reason for them to change, such as more effective collection procedures or a lengthening or shortening of credit terms.

Cash can be taken from the final balance for the end of the year on your cash budget (see above). The cash figure on your Balance Sheet will be influenced by expenditures, new loans and notes, owner's withdrawals, etc.

Items such as deposits, prepaid supplies, and prepaid expenses will probably be the same or similar, and accuracy here is not that important since these items usually make up a small percentage of total assets.

Any changes in notes or loans receivable will depend on payments made to you by debtors, and new loans or notes (again, see your cash budget).

For an inventory figure, you can use the same figure as your ending inventory the prior year unless you expect changes in the amount of inventory you will keep in stock the following year. For example, if you plan to carry an average addition of 10 percent more inventory in stock, and last year's ending inventory was $20,000, a projected ending inventory figure for next year would be $22,000 (10 percent × $20,000 = $2,000; $20,000 + $2,000 = $22,000). If sales volume increases, either your average inventory or turnover rate, or both, have to increase. Be sure your projected Balance Sheet inventory figure matches the ending inventory figure on your projected Income Statement.

Under liabilities, loans payable will be decreased by whatever payments are made during the year and increased by the amount of any new loans taken out. You must be sure to list loan payments on your cash budget. Accounts payable will probably increase proportionately as ending inventory does. Accrued liabilities for payroll, taxes, etc., will probably be about the same as the year before.

Under owner's equity, owner's capital always remains the same, unless new capital investments are made. Retained earnings will be increased by the net earnings on your projected Income Statement less owner's withdrawal.

When making your projected Balance Sheet, play around with the figures in pencil first so you can make changes. Use information from your cash budget, projected Income Statement, and prior Balance Sheet to help you arrive at projected Balance Sheet figures. Remember that total assets must match total liabilities plus owner's equity. If you add something to one side of the equation, you must add it to the other (or subtract it from another item on the same side of the equation).

SUMMING UP

Preparing a cash budget on a monthly basis is vital to the stability of a company's operation. It allows you to plan for greater cash needs during busy seasons or periods of expansion by applying for loans ahead of time. It also shows you when you will have extra cash available for short-term investments.

Projected financial statements put in writing the objectives and expectations you have for your business's future. Managerial accounting, cash budgeting, and projected financial statements are a combination approach giving you control and direction over your company's life and growth.

15
PARTNERSHIP
ACCOUNTING

If your company is a partnership, separate Capital and Withdrawal accounts must be kept for each partner. If no other agreement has been made, the law provides that all partnership earnings are to be shared equally; but the partners may agree in advance to any method of sharing earnings. If they do this, but say nothing of losses, losses are shared in the same way as earnings.

At the end of every year, your company's profits (or losses) must be distributed to each partner's Capital account. Partners, like sole proprietors, cannot actually receive a "salary" from their company. A partner works for partnership profits. You may, however, wish to allocate "salaries" or "interest" payments, or both, to partners as a way of compensating each one fairly for time and capital invested in the business. Two methods of distributing profits are discussed below, but the same principles can be applied to any method you choose.

FRACTIONAL BASIS OF ALLOCATING EARNINGS

The easiest way to divide partnership earnings is to assign each partner a fraction, equal or otherwise. For example, two partners could take one half each, one quarter and three quarters, two thirds and one third, etc. You may wish to make an unequal distribution if one partner contributes a greater share of the starting capital, or contributes more time to the business's operation.

For example, let us assume Smith and Jones have a partnership in which Smith contributed $20,000 and Jones $10,000 starting capital. Smith is managing the business full time and Jones works for it three quarters of the time. They decide to divide earnings two thirds to Smith, and one third to Jones.

When the $30,000 is invested, the Owner's Capital accounts will show the following:

SMITH CAPITAL		JONES CAPITAL	
debit (−)	credit (+)	debit (−)	credit (+)
	20,000		10,000

(Note: Cash will have been debited with the $30,000.)

At the end of the year, Smith and Jones Company has earned $9,000 profit. It will be distributed as follows:

$$\frac{2}{3} \times \$9,000 = \$6,000 \text{ to Smith}$$
$$\frac{1}{3} \times \$9,000 = \$3,000 \text{ to Jones}$$

If no withdrawals were made during the year, the total $9,000 would be credited to Smith and Jones Capital accounts as follows:

SMITH CAPITAL		JONES CAPITAL	
debit (−)	credit (+)	debit (−)	credit (+)
	20,000 *		10,000 *
	6,000		3,000

* Prior entry.

If withdrawals had been made by the partners during the year, they would be debited to Owner's Withdrawal accounts and subtracted from net profits at the end of the year:

Net profit: $9,000

Smith's share:	$6,000
less owner's withdrawal:	4,000
	$2,000 Smith's share

Jones' share:	$3,000
less owner's withdrawal:	2,500
	$ 500 Jones' share

If the company suffers a loss, the loss would be divided in the same manner as earnings and debited to each partner's Capital account:

Net loss: $3,000

Smith's share: ⅔ × $3,000 = $2,000
Jones' share: ⅓ × $3,000 = <u> 1,000</u>
$3,000 total net loss

SMITH CAPITAL		JONES CAPITAL	
debit (−)	credit (+)	debit (−)	credit (+)
2,000 †	20,000 *	1,000 †	10,000 *

* Prior entry of capital investment.
† Partner's share of net loss.

BASE SALARIES PLUS EQUAL SHARE ON BALANCE OF PROFIT

You may wish to allow each partner a set "salary" and then divide the remainder of the profits equally. For example, suppose White, Black, and Green have a partnership in which they agree to give White a salary of $10,000, Black $12,000, and Green $14,000, and to split the balance of profits equally. The division of $39,000 net profits would be as follows:

Net profits: $39,000

Green's salary: $14,000
Black's salary: $12,000
White's salary: <u>$10,000</u>
$36,000 total salaries, leaving a
balance of $3,000 from $39,000
profits

⅓ of $3,000 = $1,000 share each of balance of profits

Green's share: $14,000 + $1,000 = $15,000
Black's share: $12,000 + $1,000 = $13,000
White's share: $10,000 + $1,000 = <u>$11,000</u>
$39,000 total profits

The $15,000, $13,000, and $11,000 minus any withdrawals would be credited to each partner's Capital account.

If only $30,000 net profits had been made, the difference between the $36,000 required for partners' salaries and the net profit would be shared equally:

225

$$\$36,000 - \$30,000 = \$6,000$$

$$\frac{\$6,000}{3} = \$2,000 \text{ deducted from each partner's earnings}$$

Green's share:	$\$14,000 - \$2,000 = \$12,000$
Black's share:	$\$12,000 - \$2,000 = \$10,000$
White's share:	$\$10,000 - \$2,000 = \underline{\$\ 8,000}$

$$\$30,000 \text{ total net profits}$$

FINANCIAL STATEMENTS

A partnership Income Statement would look the same as a proprietor's (see Chapter 12) except that the distribution of profits or losses between partners would be listed at the bottom of the statement. Figure 15.1 gives an example of a partnership Income Statement. On the Balance Sheet, partners' Capital accounts are listed separately under partners' equity, as illustrated in Figure 15.2.

LOANS MADE BY PARTNERS TO A PARTNERSHIP

If a partner makes a loan to the partnership, the interest paid on this loan is a deductible business expense for the company, but must be included by the partner as part of his income. Even if the partner does not actually take the earned interest out of the company, it must be treated as an accrued expense by the partnership and declared as earnings by the partner.

For example, suppose Green loans his company $5,000 on a short-term note at eight-percent interest. In six months the company pays him the $5,000 plus $200 interest ($5,000 × eight percent × one half year). The loan and repayment would be recorded as follows:

(a) loan of $5,000 made by Green.
(b) $5,200 loan plus interest paid to Green.

CASH		LOANS PAYABLE		INTEREST EXPENSE	
debit (+)	credit (−)	debit (−)	credit (+)	debit (+)	credit (−)
5,000 (a)	5,200 (b)	5,000 (b)	5,000 (a)	200 (b)	

INCOME STATEMENT 1/1/78 TO 12/31/78

Revenues	$60,000	
Operating Expenses		
Rent	4,800	
Utilities	1,800	
Advertising	3,200	
Insurance	600	
Supplies	3,400	
Depreciation Expense	6,000	
Miscellaneous Expense	1,200	
Total Operating Expenses		21,000
Net Earnings		$39,000

Partners' Shares

Green: Salary	14,000	
+ ⅓ balance profit	1,000	
Total share	15,000	
Less owner's withdrawals	14,000	
	1,000	Balance, Green's share
Black: Salary	12,000	
+ ⅓ balance profit	1,000	
Total share	13,000	
Less owner's withdrawals	12,000	
	1,000	Balance, Black's share
White: Salary	10,000	
+ ⅓ balance profit	1,000	
Total share	11,000	
Less owner's withdrawals	10,000	
	1,000	Balance, White's share

FIGURE 15.1 Partnership Income Statement.

If, by the end of the year, Green had not yet been paid his $200 interest, an adjustment in the company's General Journal would have to be made to account for this accrued expense (see Figure 15.3). It would then appear on the Income Statement as part of Interest Expense and on the Balance Sheet under liabilities as Accrued Interest.

BALANCE SHEET AS OF 12/31/78

Current Assets			**Liabilities**	
Cash	$ 6,000		Loans Payable	$22,500
Prepaid Supplies	400			
Prepaid Expenses	100		**Partners' Equity**	
Total Current Assets	6,500		Green's Capital	16,000
			Black's Capital	11,000
Fixed Assets			White's Capital	11,000
Equipment	60,000		Total Partners' Equity	38,000
Less Accumulated				
Depreciation	6,000			
Total Fixed Assets	54,000			
Total Assets	$60,500		**Partners' Equity + Liabilities**	$60,500

FIGURE 15.2 Balance Sheet for the partners in Figure 15.1.

228

GENERAL JOURNAL   Page _1_

	date	description	debit	credit
1	13 31	Interest Expense	200	
2		Accrued Interest		200
3		To account for Interest		
4		Owed Green on $5,000 loan		
5				
6				
7				
8				
9				
10				
11				
12				
13				
14				
15				
16				
17				
18				
19				
20				

FIGURE 15.3 General Journal entry to make an adjustment for the accrued interest owed a partner on a loan.

INCOME TAXES

Like a proprietorship, a partnership as a business entity is not subject to federal and, in most cases, to state income taxes. The individual partners, however, are taxed on their share of the net earnings of the business. There is a special partnership form (Form 1065), which must be filed by the partnership. Schedule K and K-1 shows the partner's share of income, credits, deductions, etc. (See publication 334, *Tax Guide for Small Business* for complete instructions on filling out these forms and accompanying schedules.)

SUMMING UP

In partnership accounting, each partner's capital investment must be recorded in a separate capital account. At the end of the year, each partner's share of the net profits (or losses) is computed and added to or deducted from his Capital account.

229

The interest paid or accrued on loans made by partners to the business is recorded in an Interest Expense account. This interest is an allowable business expense for the partnership, but must be included as part of the partner's earnings for the year, even if the interest amount has not actually been withdrawn from the business by the partner.

Each partner's share of net earnings is taxed as individual income. There are no federal income taxes to pay as a business entity. Special partnership forms, however, must be filed which show the business's profits (or losses) and how they were distributed to the partners. Just as a proprietor would, partners pay taxes on all earnings of the business whether or not they actually withdraw these funds for personal use.

16
INTERNAL
CONTROL

The purpose of internal control procedures is to limit errors, promote efficient operation, and protect your business's assets from waste, fraud, and theft. If you are running a one-person operation in which you do everything yourself—make purchases, receive goods, make payments, etc.—you will be in control. As your business grows, however, and the number of employees increases, it will become more difficult for you personally to oversee all these functions.

This chapter covers several internal control procedures in basic areas such as purchases, receipts, and disbursements. The procedures you use will depend on the type of business you have and on its size. The principles of good internal control are as follows:

1. The clear establishment of each employee's responsibility. For example, if two people have access to the petty cash box and an error is found, it will be difficult to ascertain who is responsible for the error.
2. The maintenance of adequate records and following the recordkeeping procedures outlined throughout this book in a timely manner.
3. Obtaining adequate casualty insurance on your assets.
4. Dividing duties in the recordkeeping and maintenance of assets in a particular area. For example, you should not have the same employee placing purchase orders, receiving merchandise, and paying vendors.

5. If possible, the rotation of employees in their job functions.
6. The use of mechanical devices such as cash registers, check protectors, and mechanical counters whenever feasible.
7. Employee cooperation, obtained by explaining internal control procedures and why they are necessary.
8. The review of internal control procedures periodically in order to see that they are being followed or, if necessary, that they are changed. (For example, ask yourself, "If I were a dishonest employee, how would I go about stealing from my company?")

CASH RECEIPTS AND SALES

In a retail or service operation, you may wish to use prenumbered sales slips. You can then instruct employees to mark a slip "void" if an error is made and to keep a copy of it. At the end of the day, no numbers should be missing. If you do not follow this procedure, an employee can easily destroy a sales slip and pocket the cash. Using a cash register with a locked-in tape is another way to keep a permanent record of each cash sale.

If you receive checks in the mail from customers, it is wise to separate the processing duties and have different employees

1. Open the mail.
2. List the checks received.
3. Make bank deposits.
4. Update accounts receivable records.

A type of fraud that can occur if these duties are not separated is called "lapping receivables." A clerk takes the check from A Company and cashes it himself. The next day when B Company's check is received, he credits this payment to A Company's account. The next day when C Company's check is received, he credits this payment to B Company's account, and so forth. This way it takes a long time to uncover his theft.

When shipping goods to customers, you should establish the following procedures:

1. Use prenumbered invoices.
2. Make sure everything shipped was billed to the customer and that everything billed was shipped.
3. Do not have the same person prepare invoices, ship merchandise, and bill the customer.

232

4. Require backup material such as bills of lading, UPS receipts, etc., to prove shipment before customers are billed.

If you have an outside sales force or use commissioned sales representatives, do not allow them to collect checks, but rather have customers send checks to you directly and be sure your company address is on invoices. When a sales representative sends you a customer's order, send out a confirming order directly to the customer before shipping any merchandise. This single procedure would have saved one company $3,000 in losses from a crooked sales representative who sent in phony orders from nonexistent customers and had merchandise delivered to his own P.O. box numbers in several places.

DISBURSEMENTS

When making purchases the following procedures will assure good control:

1. Use prenumbered purchase orders as shown in Chapter 3.
2. When bills come in for purchases, match the invoice with your purchase order.
3. Compare to see that you received merchandise and that prices are correct.
4. Refoot totals, discount computations, etc.
5. Make sure shipping charges are in line.
6. If at all possible, personally approve each bill for payment.
7. Always pay bills from invoices, not statements.
8. Attach invoices to appropriate statements and check for errors.
9. Mark invoices "paid" to avoid duplicate payment.

If an employee is authorized to sign checks, you should have a different employee authorize bills for payment, or do it yourself. You should also advise your bank of a limit for which employees may cash checks. If you set no limit, you may be liable for any amount, not only what you have in your account.

If you have a petty cash fund (see Chapter 9), you should make sure only one person has access to it, and personally approve each expenditure with your signature on a petty cash slip. If you want an employee to be authorized to do this, it should be a different employee from the one controlling the cash. You should avoid using petty cash funds for such things as paying temporary labor. In one company, whenever the employee in charge of petty cash needed extra cash, she made up a chit for a "day laborer" who did not exist and pocketed the cash. Her petty cash slips were not authorized individually, and were only reviewed when she needed to reimburse the petty cash fund. By then, her occasional phony slips were undetected among the many for "day laborers."

233

INVENTORY CONTROL

As discussed in Chapters 5 and 6, keeping a perpetual inventory will help you maintain control over it. When you take a physical inventory, compare it with the perpetual records. Differences could mean recording errors or theft.

Depending on the size and nature of your inventory, you may want a simple or elaborate system of control. Certainly, your company's stock should not be available to any employee without some form of control involving responsible authorization.

SUMMING UP

You may feel that the emphasis in this chapter has been on distrusting your employees. The facts are, however, that shoddy controls *encourage* employees to steal. There are times when personal financial pressures combined with clear-cut opportunity will change an ordinarily honest employee into a thief. Then there are those who *look* for ways to increase their "take home pay."

The honest employee will be grateful for a well-run, efficient system in which to work. There is no need for a suspicious attitude on your part if you have established a good internal control system. And since your life's investment may be at stake, make sure you do it.

17

FORMS

AND

SYSTEMS

There are many forms and systems on the market—from columnar paper to electronic computers—which can help you accomplish your accounting procedures with speed and efficiency. Depending on the size of your business and the volume of recordkeeping, you may find one or more of the forms and systems described below applicable to your business.

BASIC TOOLS

You could handle all your recordkeeping with such simple tools as a piece of paper, a pencil, and your brain. Today most businesses, however, rely on other equipment such as adding machines, cash registers, and electronic calculators. The adding machine or calculator will save a lot of the time spent in adding, subtracting, etc. Cash registers are available in many models and prices, depending on what they can do. There are sophisticated electronic registers available today that can be tied directly into a computer for inventory control and other functions.

Basic paper forms for recordkeeping include analysis pads, columnar sheets, ledger sheets, post binders, ledger outfits, columnar books, account books, payroll and time records, order books, and receipt books. Other business forms you may use are invoices, purchase orders, statements, sales forms, etc.

These supplies can be purchased at your local stationers. If you cannot find what you want there, or prefer to order by mail, write to the following companies for catalogs:

Better Records
National Blank Book Co., Inc.
Holyoke, Mass. 01040

Mattick Business Forms, Inc.
333 W. Hintz Rd., Box P
Wheeling, Il. 60090

Regent Standard Forms, Inc.
5117 Central Highway
Airport Industrial Park
Pennsauken, N.J. 08109

Watts Business Forms, Inc.
Division of Lewis Bus. Forms, Inc.
Dillsburg, Pa. 17019

New England Business Service, Inc.
Townsend, Mass. 01469

SIMPLIFIED ACCOUNTING SYSTEMS

There are on the market prepared forms and systems that are set up to simplify your recordkeeping procedures by providing an organized system of recording and eliminating some of the writing steps.

Data Management, Inc., of Farmington, Connecticut, offers complete sets of looseleaf systems and supplies for bookkeeping. Figures 17.1, 17.2, and 17.3 illustrate three of the many forms available from Data Management, Inc.: (1) an annual payroll summary, (2) a capital and loan payment control sheet, and (3) an equipment cost worksheet. (Write to Data Management, Inc., for complete information on their looseleaf systems and supplies.)

There are several systems on the market that are designed to eliminate some of the writing steps in recordkeeping. For example, as you write a payroll check and stub, the information will be transferred through carbon backings to both an individual and total payroll summary. There are disbursement systems in which the check, check stub, remittance advice, disbursements journal, distribution,

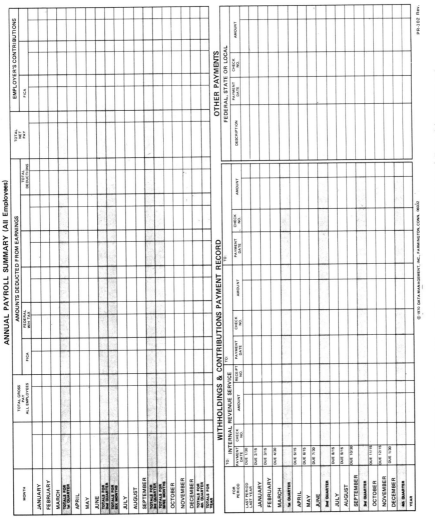

FIGURE 17.1 Annual Payroll Summary Form, available from Data Management, Inc., of Farmington, Connecticut.

237

CAPITAL AND LOAN PAYMENTS CONTROL

DETAILED BREAKDOWN OF PAYMENTS ON LOANS AND CAPITAL ITEMS

19____

HOLDER OF NOTE												
IDENTIFICATION												
												TOTALS
ACTUAL FUNDS RECEIVED OR BALANCE TO BE FINANCED												
TOTAL FINANCE CHARGE												
TOTAL AMOUNT TO BE REPAID												
DATE 1st PAYMENT												
PAYMENT DUE DATE												
PAYMENT AMOUNT												
NUMBER OF PAYMENTS												
BAL. DUE START OF YR.												
JANUARY												
FEBRUARY												
MARCH												
APRIL												
MAY												
JUNE												
JULY												
AUGUST												
SEPTEMBER												
OCTOBER												
NOVEMBER												
DECEMBER												
TOTAL PAYMENTS THIS YEAR												
BAL. DUE END OF YEAR												

(row label: S T N E M Y A P — "PAYMENTS")

INTEREST

FORM G 604

FIGURE 17.2 Capital and Loan Payment Control Sheet, available from Data Management, Inc., of Farmington, Connecticut.

238

EQUIPMENT COST WORKSHEET (MONTH BASIS)

FIGURE 17.3 Equipment Cost Worksheet, available from Data Management, Inc., of Farmington, Connecticut.

and mailing envelope are all produced in one operation, and proved in one operation. There are similar systems for billing and receipts.

Figure 17.4 shows Shaw-Walker's payroll plan for firms that have five to 40 employees. Figure 17.5 shows their checkbook disbursements plan. For more information, write to

Shaw-Walker Company
54 Park Avenue
Newark, N.J. 07102

Other simplified accounting systems include: *Write It Once* from Burroughs Corp.; Peg-Rite from Master-Craft Corp.; and Safeguard Business Systems. They all use the same principle of writing an entry once which goes through carboned forms to various other records. For information on these systems, write to

Safeguard Business Systems
Lansdale, Pa., Los Angeles, Chicago, Atlanta

Master-Craft Corp.
831 Cobb Ave.
Kalamazoo, Mich. 49007

450 James P. Rodgers Dr.
Valdosta, Ga. 31601

12804 South Spring St.
Los Angeles, Ca. 90061

Burroughs Corp.
Business Forms and Supplies Group
1150 University Ave.
Rochester, New York

You may be able to find local offices for the above companies in your phone book.

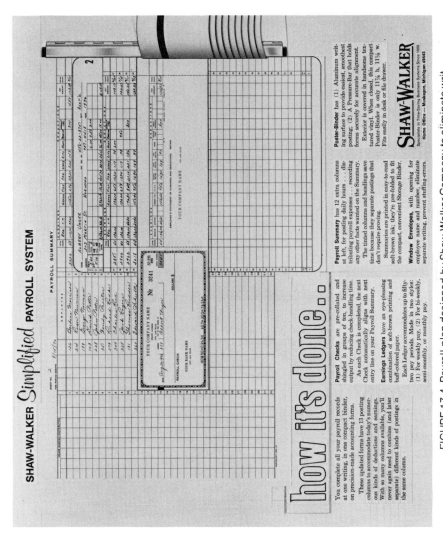

FIGURE 17.4 Payroll plan designed by Shaw-Walker Company to eliminate writing steps in recordkeeping.

241

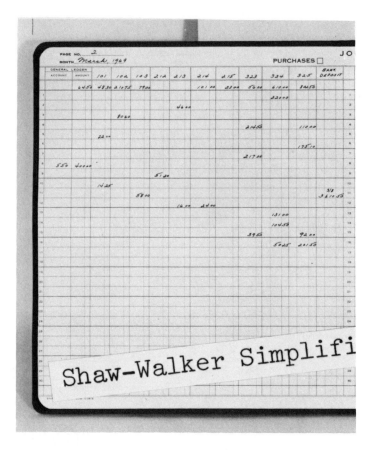

FIGURE 17.5 Checkbook Disbursements Plan designed by Shaw-Walker Company to eliminate writing steps in recordkeeping.

INVENTORY CONTROL SYSTEMS

E-Z Way Systems manufactures inventory control systems ranging from 500 card to 18,000 card capacities (see sample cards in Figure 17.6). Their systems are effective in manually operated systems for inventory, production, tool room, maintenance, etc. For more information, write to

> E-Z Way Systems
> Div. Industrial Automative, Inc.
> Box No. 700
> Newark, Ohio 43055

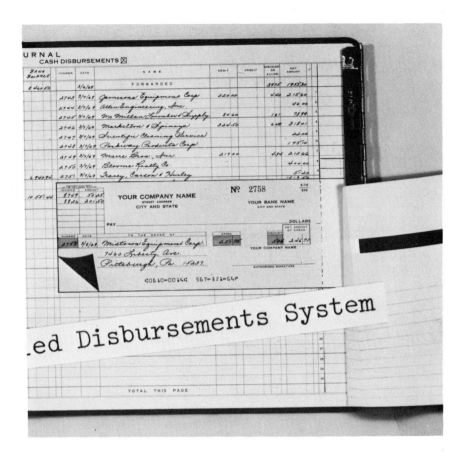

ELECTRONIC DATA PROCESSING

Depending on the size of your company and the volume of recordkeeping and paper processing you require, you may or may not find it profitable to use some sort of electronic data processing equipment. Before making a decision to purchase such a system, you should consider present bookkeeping labor costs; initial start-up costs for the system; labor costs to operate the system; dollar value benefits the system will provide; etc. An interim step might be to use a time-sharing service initially. This may be less costly, especially if you do not generate enough work to use a computer system full time.

PART NUMBER			DESCRIPTION						STOCK LOCATION			

SOURCE		SOURCE PART NO.		PRICING PER _____		

REPLACES		STD. PKG.	WEIGHT PER _____	SHIP VIA		ECONOMICAL ORDER	REORDER POINT	REORDER QTY.

REPLACED BY	1	2	3	4	5	6	7	8	9	10	11	12	YEAR	TOTAL

PURCHASES **DISBURSEMENTS**

DATE	P.O. NO.	ORDER	RECD.	DATE	REFERENCE	IN	OUT	BAL.	DATE	REFERENCE	IN	OUT	BAL.	DATE	REFERENCE	IN	OUT	BAL.

ORDERED TO BE | FORM 2-4 | PART NO. | E-Z-WAY SYSTEMS © NEWARK, OH 43055 LITHO IN U.S.A. | ORDERED TO BE

BACKORDER CARD

QUANTITY _____ PART NUMBER _____ MFG. _____

CUSTOMER
OR _____
USAGE _____
_____

DATE _____ PUR. ORDER
OR _____
REQUISITION
NUMBER

REMARKS _____
_____
_____

FILE THIS BACKORDER CARD PRECEDING THE CORRESPONDING
INVENTORY CONTROL CARD
IF THIS NUMBER IS NOT A STOCK ITEM, FILE THIS CARD
NUMERICALLY WITH INVENTORY CONTROL CARDS

OUR ORDER
NUMBER _____ DATE _____

ORDERED
FROM _____
_____
_____

REMARKS _____
_____
_____
_____

ORDER NO | FORM 3-1 | PART NO. | ORDER NO

FIGURE 17.6 Sample inventory cards are to be used with E-Z Way Systems inventory control systems.

With the rapid growth of technology in this field, especially the emergence of the low-cost minicomputer and microcomputer, it is hard to say exactly what hardware may be available on the market when you read this book. You might contact several manufacturers and ask for a demonstration of their latest models.

Three models presently on the market are described below to give you an idea of what these machines can do.

Monroe, The Calculator Company, has a Model 200 Electronic Billing System which they claim will reduce billing time by at least 50 percent. It combines the flexibility and accuracy of a computer with the speed, ease, and legibility of a typewriter. In processing invoices, it

1. Spaces to the proper column automatically.
2. Automatically types the date and invoice number.
3. Converts any pricing or quantity factor automatically.
4. Computes discounts.
5. Automatically computes and types taxes.
6. Accurately figures final totals.

A newer model (200-1) will even provide an error-free method of posting to customer ledger cards and simultaneously typing statements.

Olivetti Model A-4 was designed expressly for accounting and business administration. It is a general-purpose machine for accounts, stock control, payroll, invoicing, banking, and data collection. It consists of

1. A central unit for arithmetic/logic operations and data and program storage.
2. A programming unit.
3. A keyboard for entering data and operating commands.
4. A print unit and carriage for journals, continuous stationery, ledger cards, and individual forms.

The A-4 is a fast, flexible, desk-top accounting/invoice machine, but at the same time is also a complete four-operation calculator.

NCR Corporation's Model 299 Electronic Accounting System is pictured in Figure 17.7. The NCR 299 expedites the basic accounting functions to their final destination in General Ledger and management reports; it expedites high-volume and specialized jobs, such as billing and payroll; and it summarizes the data and prepares the financial and management reports. Some of the specialized application areas are as follows:

Retailing
    cycle billing
    inventory control

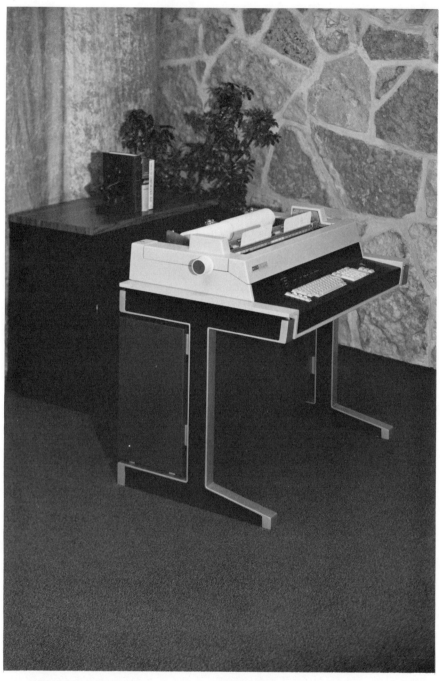

FIGURE 17.7 NCR Corporation Model 299 Electronic Accounting System. Photo courtesy of NCR Corporation, Dayton, Ohio 45479.

Wholesaling
　　order billing
　　sales analysis

Manufacturing
　　job cost
　　work in process
　　work-center loading
　　efficiency reporting

Contractors
　　estimating
　　job costing
　　equipment records
　　daily labor reporting

SUMMING UP

Once you understand the principles and procedures of accounting, you will want to set up the simplest, most efficient system you can. You should take advantage of the forms and systems on the market to save recordkeeping costs, improve accuracy, and provide the necessary feedback for management decisions.

Even if your business is very small, there are manual forms and systems that are inexpensive and will improve the organization and efficiency of your accounting records. Whether or not an electronic accounting system will pay for itself in your company depends on the amount of processing you do and the volume of your business. Time-sharing, minicomputers, or microcomputers may be the answer for you.

SUMMARY
OF
ACCOUNTING
PROCEDURES

This summary lists each accounting procedure and the frequency (daily, weekly, monthly, etc.) with which it should be done. Items are separated by topic, with the applicable chapters referenced. Using this Summary as a guide, set up a calendar listing important procedures that must be done on certain days, such as filing a tax form or taking a trial balance for your company.

JOURNALS AND LEDGERS (CHAPTER 2)

1. Daily list checks written in Cash Disbursements Journal.
2. Daily list incoming cash and checks in Cash Receipts Journal.
3. Monthly post entries from Cash Disbursements Journal, Cash Receipts Journal, Sales Journal, Purchases Journal, Payroll Book, and General Journal to General Ledger.

PURCHASES (CHAPTER 3)

1. *Cash Basis.* Daily list payments for purchases in Cash Disbursements Journal. Post to General Ledger monthly as debit to Purchases Expense, credit to Cash.
2. *Modified Accrual Method.* Daily list payments for purchases in Cash Disbursements Journal as in cash method. Make an end-of-the-year adjustment in General Journal for unpaid invoices. Post as debit to Purchases Expense, credit to Accounts Payable. Reverse this entry at the beginning of the following year.
3. *Strict Accrual Method.* Daily or weekly record invoices as received in Purchases Journal. Post as credit to Accounts Payable, debit to Purchases Expense. Record payments in Cash Disbursements Journal. Post as debit to Accounts Payable, credit to Cash.
4. *Accounts Payable Subsidiary Ledger.* Daily or weekly post entries from Purchases Journal as credits, entries from Cash Disbursements Journal as debits. Monthly or quarterly take a trial balance of subsidiary ledger and agree (or reconcile) to General Ledger account.

SALES AND ACCOUNTS RECEIVABLE (CHAPTER 4)

1. *Cash Basis.* Daily list all receipts from customers in Cash Receipts Journal. Post as debit to Cash and credit to Sales or Revenues.
2. *Accrual Basis.* File invoices numerically and staple tape of monthly total to front of Sales folder. To break sales down by departments or product lines, record invoices in Sales Journal. Post monthly totals as debit to Accounts Receivable and credit to Sales.
3. *Subsidiary Ledger.* Post weekly or monthly. Post entries from Sales folder or Sales Journal as debits. Post entries from Cash Receipts Journal as credits. Take aged trial balance monthly and reconcile to General Ledger account.

RETAIL STORE (CHAPTER 5)

1. Prepare Daily Summary each day.
2. Transfer Daily Summary totals to Cash Receipts Journal daily or weekly.
3. *Inventory.* Take physical inventory *at least* once a year. If you keep perpetual inventory records, compare with physical inventory at least once a year. You may estimate your inventory value using the retail inventory method.

MANUFACTURING (CHAPTER 6)

1. Separate manufacturing labor and overhead costs from sales and administrative labor and overhead costs. Do this before preparing financial statements (monthly, quarterly, or yearly).
2. Take and cost physical inventory at least once a year. If you keep perpetual inventory records, compare with physical inventory at least once a year.

FIXED ASSETS (CHAPTER 7)

1. When you purchase a machine, vehicle, etc., record on Fixed Assets Purchases Schedule and in Cash Disbursements Journal.
2. Compute depreciation on fixed assets at least once a year prior to preparing financial statements. Make a General Journal entry debiting Depreciation Expense and crediting Accumulated Depreciation.

MISCELLANEOUS ASSETS AND LIABILITIES (CHAPTER 8)

1. *Loans Receivable.* When you loan money, as in employee advances, list payment in Cash Disbursements Journal. Post as credit to Cash, debit to Employee Advances. When employee pays you back, record in Cash Receipts Journal. Post as debit to Cash and credit to Employee Advances.
2. *Notes Receivable.* When note is received in place of accounts receivable, record in General Journal as debit to Notes Receivable and credit to Accounts Receivable. When payment is made, record in Cash Receipts Journal and post as debit to Cash and credit to Notes Receivable.
3. *Deposits.* When you pay deposits for rent, telephone, gas and electric, etc., record in Cash Disbursements Journal. Post as debit to Deposits and credit to Cash. When deposit is refunded, record in Cash Receipts Journal. Post as debit to Cash and credit to Deposits.
4. *Loans Payable.* When you borrow money, record in Cash Receipts Journal. Post as debit to Cash and credit to Loans Payable. When you make a payment on a loan, record in Cash Disbursements Journal. Post total as credit to Cash. Post payment on principle as debit to Loans Payable. Post interest payment as debit to Interest Expense.
5. *Accrued Expenses.* (Ignore if you are on the cash basis of accounting for tax purposes.) At the end of the year, record accrued expenses in General Journal. Post as debit to expense account and credit to the appropriate "payables" ac-

251

count. At beginning of following year, reverse entry—debit "payables" account and credit expense account.

6. *Deferred Revenues.* At the end of the year, record deferred revenues in General Journal. Post as debit to Sales or Revenues and credit to Deferred Revenues. At beginning of following year, reverse entry—debit Deferred Revenues and credit Sales or Revenues.

CASH (CHAPTER 9)

1. *Change Fund.* To set up a change fund, write a check for amount of the fund and cash it. Record in Cash Disbursements Journal. Post as debit to Change Fund and credit to Cash.

2. *Petty Cash Fund.* To set up a petty cash fund, write check for amount of fund and cash it. Record in Cash Disbursements Journal. Post as debit to Petty Cash Fund and credit to Cash. When petty cash is spent, fill out petty cash slip. When reimbursing petty cash fund, write check for total of slips and record in Cash Disbursements Journal, itemizing accounts to be charged. Post as debit to expense accounts and credit to Cash.

3. *Bank Statement.* When you receive your monthly bank statement, check for accuracy, then reconcile with your monthly checkbook balance and your General Ledger Cash account balance.

4. *Recording Bank Deposits.* You can add a "deposit" column to your Cash Receipts Journal. Whenever you make a bank deposit, list the amount in this column. Deposit cash receipts daily or weekly.

PAYROLL (CHAPTER 10)

1. When you hire employees, have them fill out W-4 or W-4E forms, plus city state withholding certificates.

2. Compute and record employee wages, withholding and FICA taxes in payroll book.

3. When you pay employees, write a check for net amount and give employee itemized statement (or use payroll checks with itemized stubs).

4. If required by law, make monthly deposits of taxes withheld plus employer's share of FICA to qualified commercial bank or Federal Reserve Bank. Use Tax Deposit Form 501.

5. Quarterly file federal Form 941 with balance of withholding and FICA taxes due. File and pay state (and city) unemployment and withholding taxes if required.

6. Yearly file and pay federal unemployment taxes. Supply employees with W-2 yearly summaries and send copies to city, state, and federal governments.

7. *Recording Payroll Expenses*

Cash basis. When salaries are paid, tax payments made, etc., record in Cash Disbursements Journal. Post as debits to Payroll Expense and credit to Cash.

Modified accrual. Record as in Cash method. At end of year make adjustment in General Journal for all salaries and taxes owed for work performed prior to the end of the year. Post as debit to Payroll Expense and credit to Salaries and Taxes Payable. At the beginning of the following year, reverse entry—debit Salaries and Taxes Payable and credit Payroll Expense.

Strict accrual. From payroll book, post net salaries as debit to Salaries Expense and credit to Payroll Clearing Account. Post deductions from employee's salary as debit to Salaries Expense and credit to Payroll Taxes Payable. Post employer's share of FICA as debit to Payroll Tax Expense and credit to Payroll Taxes Payable.

From Cash Disbursements Journal, post net salaries paid as debit to Payroll Clearing Account and credit to Cash. Post tax payments as debit to Payroll Taxes Payable and credit to Cash.

Owner's salaries

Corporation: Treat as employee's salary, deducting taxes, etc.

Proprietorship: Record money taken out of business by owner in Cash Disbursements Journal. Post as debit to Owner's Withdrawal and credit to Cash.

Partnership: Record money taken out of business by partners in separate withdrawal accounts for each partner.

8. *Workers' Compensation and Disability Insurance.* Record payments in Cash Disbursements Journal. Post as debit to Insurance Expense or Payroll Expense and credit to Cash.

SALES AND USE TAXES (CHAPTER 11)

1. Apply for Seller's Permit from state government.
2. Collect sales taxes from customers where required by law.
3. File returns and pay sales and use taxes monthly or quarterly as required by law.
4. *Recording Sales and Use Tax Payments*

Cash basis. When you pay sales and use taxes, record in Cash Disbursements Journal. Post as debit to Sales and Use Tax Expense and credit to Cash.

Accrual basis. Use cash method and make an end-of-the year adjustment in General Journal for taxes owed on sales made prior to the end of the year. Post as debit to Sales and Use Tax Expense and credit to Sales and Use Taxes Payable. At the beginning of the following year, reverse adjustment—debit Sales and Use Taxes Payable and credit Sales and Use Tax Expense.

PREPARING FINANCIAL STATEMENTS (CHAPTER 12)

1. Take a trial balance of General Ledger accounts every month.
2. At end of year, make any necessary adjustments or accruals, or both, in "adjustments" column on Trial Balance Worksheet. If retail, wholesale, or manufacturing concern, make adjustment to Cost of Goods Sold and Inventory.
3. Total "General Ledger balance" columns and "adjustments" columns to get "Adjusted Trial Balance" columns.
4. Separate Income Statement and Balance Sheet figures on Trial Balance Worksheet.
5. Add difference between Net Profit and Owner's Withdrawal to Retained Earnings.
6. Prepare Income Statement and Balance Sheet.
7. Close out Income Statement accounts.
8. Beginning of following year, reverse accruals.

CASH BUDGETING AND FINANCIAL PLANNING (CHAPTER 14)

1. Prepare a cash budget showing expected cash in, cash out, and balance for each month. Prepare for three months, six months, or a year in advance.
2. Revise cash budget as necessary from month to month.
3. Prepare a projected Income Statement for the coming year.
4. Prepare a projected Balance Sheet for the coming year.

PARTNERSHIP ACCOUNTING (CHAPTER 15)

1. Compute each partner's share of profits on a monthly or yearly basis.
2. Record partners' share of profits in separate Capital accounts.
3. On partner's loans to partnership, record interest payments or interest accrued as Interest Expense whether or not partner has actually taken money out of the business. This interest will be taxed as part of partner's individual income.
4. At end of year, file partnership Form 1065 and accompanying schedules with IRS.

BIBLIOGRAPHY

Nickerson, Clarence B. *Accounting Handbook for Non-Accountants*. Boston: Cahners Books, 1975.

Pyle, William W. and White, John Arch. *Fundamental Accounting Principles*. Homewood, Ill.: Richard D. Irwin, Inc., 1972.

Ragan, Robert C. *Financial Recordkeeping for Small Stores*. Washington, D.C.: Small Business Administration, 1966.

Spiller, Earl A., Sr. *Financial Accounting—Basic Concepts*. Homewood, Ill.: Richard D. Irwin, Inc., 1971.

Taetzsch, Lyn. *Opening Your Own Retail Store*. Chicago: Henry Regnery Company Publishers, 1976.

Taetzsch, Lyn and Genfan, Herb. *How to Start Your Own Craft Business*. New York: Watson-Guptill Publishers, 1974.

Welsch, Glenn A., Zlatkovich, Charles T., White, John Arch. *Intermediate Accounting*. Homewood, Ill.: Richard D. Irwin, Inc., 1972.

Wick, Jack Z. *A Handbook of Small Business Finance*. Washington, D.C.: Small Business Administration, 1965.

INDEX